THE POLITICAL ECONOMY OF TRANSITION IN CENTRAL AND EASTERN EUROPE

T0382769

For the woman and girl in my life,

Kalliope and Regilla

The Political Economy of Transition in Central and Eastern Europe

The light(s) at the end of the tunnel

Edited by
JENS BASTIAN
The London School of Economics and Political Science
European Institute

Routledge
Taylor & Francis Group

LONDON AND NEW YORK

First published 1998 by Ashgate Publishing

Reissued 2018 by Routledge
2 Park Square, Milton Park, Abingdon, Oxon, OX14 4RN
711 Third Avenue, New York, NY 10017, USA

Routledge is an imprint of the Taylor & Francis Group, an informa business

Publisher's Note
The publisher has gone to great lengths to ensure the quality of this reprint but points out that some imperfections in the original copies may be apparent.

Disclaimer
The publisher has made every effort to trace copyright holders and welcomes correspondence from those they have been unable to contact.

A Library of Congress record exists under LC control number: 98073760

ISBN 13: 978-1-138-34442-6 (hbk)
ISBN 13: 978-1-138-34444-0 (pbk)
ISBN 13: 978-0-429-43850-9 (ebk)

Contents

Tables

List of contributors

Jens Bastian is a DAAD Lecturer in the Political Economy of Transition at the *London School of Economics*, European Institute. He received his Ph.D. from the *European University Institute* in Florence, Italy. Prior to his engagement at the London School of Economics he worked as a Research Fellow at *Nuffield College*, Center for European Studies, Oxford.

Péter Á. Bod is Research Professor of Economics and Finance at *Veszprém University, Hungary*. He was formerly *Minister of Industry and Trade* in the first democratically elected Hungarian government of 1990-91, and subsequently *Governor of the National Bank of Hungary*. Between 1995 and 1998 he was an Executive Director of the *European Bank for Reconstruction and Development*, London.

Anne-Ev Enzmann is currently working with *A.T. Kearney*, an international management consulting company. She received her Master degree from the *College of Europe* Bruges – Warsaw in 1995. Between 1995 and 1996 she conducted an international project on assistance, business and consultancy in Central and Eastern Europe, which was sponsored by the *Robert Bosch Foundation* in Germany.

Nadja Hahn is currently working as a trainee reporter for *Bloomberg Business News* in London. She received her Master degree in the Political Economy of Transition in Europe in 1997 at the *London School of Economics*. In 1996 she completed her Bachelor of Arts in international relations at *Boston University*.

Piotr Jaworski completed his MA in Economics at *Warsaw School of Economics* in 1995. He received his Master degree in the Political Economy of Transition in Europe in 1997 at the *London School of Economics*. Between 1988 and 1990 he was a member of the *Wroclaw Town Council*. He currently holds a teaching position at the *Institute of Economics II* of the *Warsaw School of Economics*.

Gudrun Lingner is a free-lance journalist working for various newspapers in Paris, France and Bonn, Germany. During 1996 she worked as a journalist in Romania where she conducted a comparison between the newspapers *Adevarul* and *România Libera*. The research was sponsored by a scholarship from the *Robert Bosch Foundation* in Germany.

Ryszard Rapacki is a Reader in Economics at the *Warsaw School of Trade*. Between 1972 and 1990 he taught economics at the *Central School of Planning and Statistics*. He is currently head of the *Economics Institute II* at the *Warsaw School of Economics*. He is the author of *Poland into the 1990s. Economy and Society in Transition*, Pinter Publishers, London 1991.

Abbreviations

APS	Asociatia Presei Sportive
APT	Asociatia Profesionistilor din Televiziune
AWS	Akcja Wyborcza Solidarnosc / Electoral Action Solidarity
AZR	Asociatia Ziaristilor din România
BSP	Bulgarian Socialist Party
CAP	Common Agriculture Policy
CDU	Christian Democratic Union
CEE	Central and Eastern Europe
CMEA/	
COMECON	Council of Mutual Economic Assistance
CPI	Consumer Price Index
CPRF	Communist Party of the Russian Federation
CURS	Center for Urban and Regional Sociology, Bucharest
EBRD	European Bank for Reconstruction and Development
EU	European Union
FDI	Foreign Direct Investment
FKgP	Independent Smallholders' Party
GM	General Motors
GDP	Gross Domestic Product
GDR	German Democratic Republic
HDSZ	Movement for a Democratic Slovakia
IMF	International Monetary Fund
KDNP	Christian Democratic Peoples' Party

KPEiR	Polish Pensioners' Party
MDF	Hungarian Democratic Forum
MNC	Multi-National Corporation
MSZDP	Social Democratic Party of Hungary
MSZMP	Hungarian Socialist Workers' Party
MZSP	Hungarian Socialist Party
NKVD	Stalin's Secret Service
OECD	Organization for Economic Cooperation and Development
PDS	Party of Democratic Socialism
PDSR	Romanian Party of Democratic Socialism
PSL	Polskie Stonnictwo Ludowe / Polish Peasant Party
PZPR	United Polish Workers Party
RCP	Romanian Communist Party
R&D	Research and Development
SdRP	Social-democratic Party of Poland
SED	Socialist Unity Party
SLD	Sojusz Lewicy Demokratycznej / Democratic Left Alliance
SME	Small and Medium sized Enterprises
SOEs	State Owned Enterprises
SPD	Social Democratic Party of Germany
SZDSZ	Alliance of Free Democrats
SZR	Societatea Ziaristilor din România
UDF	Union of Democratic Forces
UN	United Nations
UW	Unia Wolnosci / Freedom Union
UZPR	Uniunea Ziaristilor Profesionisti Romîni
VAT	Value Added Tax
WAZ	Westdeutsche Allgemeine Zeitung
ZCHN	Zjednoczenie Chrześcijańsko Narodowe / National Christian Union

1 Introduction

Jens Bastian

When European Union accession negotiations formerly opened in March 1998 with Poland, Hungary, the Czech Republic, Slovenia and Estonia, a symbolic milestone among countries of Central and Eastern Europe was reached. In the words of the Polish Foreign Minister, Bronislaw Geremek, anchoring these countries in the West means to "regain our natural place" (IHT 18.04.1998). The passage towards achieving this objective is anything but an 'easy ride'. Sequencing the re-integration of post-communist states into western institutions such as the EU will be a momentous challenge, while a sense of *Realpolitik* is simultaneously in high demand. Representatives such as Geremek, who survived the Nazi occupation of Poland during World War II, escaping the Warsaw ghetto at age 11 with his mother, are not a *Pollyanna*. While their determination is undaunted, the chief negotiators from the first round of applicant countries - the Czech Republic, Hungary, Poland, Slovenia and Estonia - have had to learn, at times the hard way, that they cannot expect any favors from a Union, which is itself rather painstakingly seeking institutional reform and monetary convergence ahead of Eastern enlargement. Hence, negotiations on what promises to be an arduous path to the European Union are expected to extend into the next millennium. There is no firm date for future membership in the EU, let alone in EMU.

Along this path the individual countries from Central and Eastern Europe knocking on the Union's door are in a constant process of self-assessment regarding the performance of their transition processes. This exercise in scrutinizing their political economies seeks to convey a mission statement to a variety of audiences: their respective populations, the neighboring countries and international organizations. The inquiry centres around the following issues: Where do we stand eight years after the events of 1989/90, and what "corridor of transformation" (Misztal 1996, p. 136) do we still have ahead of us? In other words, the desire to join the EU, and subsequently EMU, will impose a straitjacket in various spheres of their respective political economies. Constraints in fiscal policy-making, central banks shifting their exchange-rate regimes from currency pegs dominated by the dollar to systems more closely linked to the introduction of the *Euro*, democratic benchmarks in areas such as the treatment of ethnic minorities, as well as administrative requirements in the fields of civil service training, auditing procedures and effective budget management comprise a momentous legal, intellectual and organizational task. Such an undertacking is simultaneously becoming a disciplining device on the region's emerging markets. Economic policy makers are using prospective EU membership as planning targets, for instance in the field of convergence criteria. In short, anticipated EU membership enhances rewriting economic ground rules far beyond trade patterns and portfolio investment.

The term *political economy of transition* in this volume investigates how observed differences in institutions affect political and economic outcomes in various social, economic and political systems of Central and Eastern European countries. It also examines how the institutions themselves change and develop in response to entrenched legacies of the past, uncertainty of outcome as well as opportunity structures and manifest constraints. The political economy of transition thus discusses issues of critical importance for Central and Eastern Europe: Why does foreign direct investment matter? What determines social insurance reforms? How does the media establish its independence and affect the anchoring of liberal democracies? Are former communist parties nothing else then 'dressed-up as sheep'? The subtitle of this edited volume - *The Light(s) at the End of the Tunnel* - is an image of, and metaphor for, the contingencies of political economies in Central and Eastern Europe. Its rather favorable assertion, namely that illumination is in sight for - at least some - transition countries, is a recognition of the manifold performance achieved in post-communist societies since 1989/90. It is also an explicit statement against gloom and doom scenarios. Examples of such achievements are detailed in the various chapters, and increasingly receive the recognition they deserve. They concern, for instance, that:

(i) Europe's two fastest-growing economies (excepting those rebuilding from war) are in transition countries: Poland's economy grew by 6.9 percent in 1997 and Estonia's expanded by 8 percent. Furthermore, Poland has steadily continued to reduce inflation, from 250 percent in 1990 to almost 14 percent in mid-1998. In consequence, such performances have not gone unnoticed to European institutional investors with fixed-income funds. Polish, Hungarian and Czech markets are starting to be considered as an increasingly liquid alternative and as diversification for fund managers; but also as future members of the EU and EMU. In 1997 Hungary saw hefty foreign inflows to its stock market, helping make the Budapest Stock Exchange the world's second-best performer, after Moscow.

(ii) Central European countries are making a return to international capital markets in growing numbers. At the end of March 1998, the National Bank of Hungary placed a five-year, $300m *eurobond*. The offer was Hungary's first in US dollars since an issue of floating-rate notes in 1994 and followed a five-year, DM750m floating-rate bond issued in early 1998. The proceeds from the *eurobond* will be used for the *early* repayment of $670m of World Bank loans, thus lowering Hungary's debt servicing costs. Polish *zloty* and Czech *koruna* bonds are equally becoming part of Western European investment banks' expanding proprietary portfolio in countries of Central and Eastern Europe. Hungary's telecommunication utility *Matav Rt.* as well as the oil-and-gas concern *MOL Rt.* are rising in Western European funds' portfolios.[1]

(iii) With countries such as Poland, Hungary, Estonia and the Czech Republic establishing a strategic presence in the three main currency sectors (US dollar, German mark and the Japanese Yen), and improving their foreign exchange reserves, they are not as dependent anymore on international financial institutions (IFIs)

3

such as the World Bank, the IMF and the EBRD for financial assets.[2] Moreover, with the advent of Economic and Monetary Union gaining currency, and Poland, Hungary, the Czech Republic, Slovenia as well as Estonia beginning EU accession negotiations, bond emissions denominated in *Euros* are only a matter of time for these countries.

(iv) Given their credit ratings by international rating agencies such as *Standard & Poor's* and *Moody's*, the two leading US agencies, an increasing number of transition countries in Central and Eastern Europe can now attract more favorable credit conditions on international capital markets. *Moody's*, for instance, placed Hungary's rating on review for a possible upgrade in April 1998. It is currently rated at the lowest investment grades BBB-. However, significant improvements in budget deficit reductions, curtailment of consumer price inflation and containing current account imbalances justify a revision of credit ratings.

(v) Countries in Central and Eastern Europe must wonder at times what labels are being introduced, and [later] dropped, in order to pigeon-hole them from a Western perspective. The inflation of terminology may be as much a sign of confusion, as it illustrates the 'moving target', which observers in Washington, Paris, London, Berlin, Brussels or Tokyo are trying to make sense of. The magnitude of changes taking place in Central and East European countries invites investors and analysts to re-invent their own political and economic geography. The panoply of terms include: *post-communist, transition/transformation countries, emerging markets, fast-track countries,* and most recently, *graduate reform countries of Central and Eastern Europe.* The range of options stretches the arch even further. When US investment banks talk about *Extended Pan Europe,* they include the whole of the EU, non-European economic and monetary union members, plus Switzerland, Norway and some countries to the east of Germany.

These achievements and developments have a number of features in common. The most striking is that while Cold War divisions may persist in some politicians' minds, institutional investors are quietly - and for the most part effectively - redrawing the Continent's map as they move Central Europe out of the realm of 'emerging markets' and into the periphery of Europe proper. However, as Lord Dahrendorf has noted with a view to post-communist transition, the trajectory towards prospering market economies and stable liberal democracies "leads through a valley of tears" (Dahrendorf 1997, p. 94). In other words, the terms *transition* and *transformation* are not understood as a linear passage towards stated objectives. Rather, the variety of contributions in this volume see such processes as fraught with ambivalence in economic, political, legal, administrative, social and cultural spheres as well as coming to terms with entrenched legacies of the past. In short, contemporary policy-making in Central and Eastern Europe is characterized by contingencies, is open-ended, and includes - for the foreseeable future - numerous implementation deficits. These include, *inter alia,*

(i) Industrial production is still mainly geared towards domestic markets. Countries such as Hungary and Estonia have proven track records as open economies encouraging foreign investment, while others, such as Poland and Romania, have been more hesitant about privatization and more protective of domestic industries. As Eastern European economies become integrated with Western Europe competition is sure to increase in the internal European market, raising temptations to control market access from outside.

(ii) Inter-company indebtedness being very high, many industries are short of investment and teetering on the brink of bankruptcy. This situation is acerbated by financial systems that are frequently governed by under-capitalized state-owned banks with large amounts of bad assets and non-performing loans. Even countries with a comparatively better performance record in the political economy of transition are facing considerable challenges in their banking sector. *Komercni Banka*, for instance, the biggest Czech

5

bank by assets in 1998, raised provisions for its non-performing loans, which have increased to 30 percent of total loans. Financial structures are thus in dire need for reform. After adjustment for international standards on loan provisioning, not one of the five first-round EU applicants from Central and Eastern Europe - the Czech Republic, Hungary, Poland, Slovenia and Estonia - can boast a banking sector the size of a medium-sized Western bank.

(iii) Stock exchanges in former communist countries are under-capitalized. The Warsaw Stock Exchange, for instance, is capitalized at a mere $15 billion. Outside of Budapest's listed market, the region offers few stocks large enough for institutional investors to purchase in sizeable blocks. The portion of the debt market open to foreigners is worth about $18 billion in Poland and just $10 billion in Hungary, compared to about $100 billion in Greece. When German investors bought into Czech *koruna* bonds in early 1997 as a 'safe', high-yielding alternative to *Bunds*, they badly burned their fingers when the then Klaus government let the *koruna* drop by some 20 percent amid an economic crisis and speculative attacks on the currency.

(iv) Equity markets are underdeveloped, and transition economies offer few debt securities with maturities longer than five years. Fear of speculative 'hot money' has prompted many of the region's countries to place restrictions on foreign investment in their local debt markets. Hungary, for instance, restricts foreigners from investing in government securities with a maturity of less than a year. Trading in currency forwards and options is only possible in the Czech Republic.

(v) Existing bankruptcy regulation is often not, or half-heartedly implemented. Concerns like these risk alienating fund managers. Especially for equity markets the implementation of coherent bankruptcy provisions are essential. Where this is not the case, mainstream European fund managers see the region's markets and legislation as still too shallow, volatile, and just plain risky for long-term investment.

The contributions in this volume are subdivided into eight chapters, some of which cover similar topics from different angles. The contributions are a sample of the magnitude of the task and the ambivalence of the results achieved so far in transforming the political economy of former communist countries. The first two contributions by *Bod* and *Enzmann* address the complexities of foreign direct investment in Central and Eastern European countries. From different points of departure, they converge in the assessment that transition countries require huge sums to (re-)build the economic infrastructure of telecommunications, transport networks, energy, water and waste treatment, as well as financial services reform in banking privatization, introduction of private pension funds and liquidization of medium-term benchmark bonds. The infrastructure investment needs of the 10 EU candidate countries from Central and Eastern Europe alone have been estimated at more than *Ecu* 180bn ($197bn). Equally, the legal and administrative frameworks required to attract and absorb foreign capital have to be taken into account. Governments throughout the region are becoming more sophisticated and more aware of the competition for foreign investment. As both authors show, they are learning that foreign investment brings, and requires more than just capital. It also provides and demands technology, managerial skills and further access to global markets.

In chapter four, *Bastian* addresses one of the crucial aspects of political economies in Central and Eastern Europe: rebuilding social insurance systems. More specifically, state pension schemes are under severe resource pressures since the transitions have started in former communist countries. Finding and implementing a progressive replacement of so-called pay-as-you-go schemes has led countries such as Hungary and Poland to introduce new private, mandatory systems within a multi-pillar pension architecture. Here the aim is to either replace or combine a reformed pay-as-you-go system with mandatory private pension funds and a regulated voluntary private system. It is further argued that the multiplicity of retirement savings is one of the most important driving forces in the future evolution of capital markets in Central and Eastern Europe. The irony of the argument presented is that pension reforms being undertaken in transition economies may even be able to offer some - reluctant - Western European governments lessons in the implementation of social security reform.

The subsequent two chapters seek to turn the attention of the reader to the political, democratic features of transition countries. *Hahn* as well as *Lingner* highlight an aspect of post-communist countries whose development is a key benchmark for the consolidation of a democratic, law-based market economy and society: media reform. Crafting democracies includes the fertile ground of public information and debate about the direction, scope and normative underpinning of the changes taking place in Central and Eastern Europe. The availability of a rich variety of print media, state-sponsored and privately organized radio and television stations is a reflection of the populations in Poland, Hungary, Romania or Bulgaria engaging in, and aspiring to anchor *civitas sociales*. Such an endeavor requires new media legislation, the clarification of ownership structures, distribution provisions and a degree of internationalization. In other words, media reform in Central and Eastern Europe is essentially about media politics, and how citizens seek to regain a sphere of public involvement in matters concerning their daily livelihoods.

Jaworski and *Rapacki* focus their contribution on the country, which is considered by most observers as displaying the greatest degree of progress in the political economy of transition: Poland. Its macro-economic indicators are noteworthy. Poland is the first country to have succeeded in returning to the output levels of 1989. Furthermore, with respect to the EU enlargement process eastwards, Poland is by far the most important country in the region. Compared to the other Central and East European countries currently negotiating EU membership, Poland is larger in size (312.000 square kilometers) and population number (38.5 million) than the combined total of Estonia, Slovenia, the Czech Republic and Hungary. However, as Jaworski and Rapacki's contribution underlines, the domestic debate about Poland's 'return to Europe' is not a foregone conclusion.

The final chapter of the volume undertakes to illuminate a still rather controversial issue in the political economy of transition: the electoral successes of former Communist parties in Central and Eastern Europe. As *Bastian* argues, in some cases such parties have been voted into public office - presidencies and/or governments - in others they have subsequently been driven back to the harder benches of parliamentary opposition. Poland now has a President, who was a communist minister of sports in 1989, and a Prime Minister, who was a leading activist in the opposition *Solidarnosc* movement. To what degree former Communist parties have succeeded in comprehensive and credible change remains a matter of intense debate in East and West. For some observers this issue concerns the moral currency of transition, for others it highlights the capacity of societies to arrive at an understanding of the events leading to the *annus miraculis* in 1989/90. What is nevertheless becoming clearer in the course of the past decade is that former Communist parties and their new representatives reflect a variety of avenues that is as diverse as the routes of transition. Although generalizations may easily invite themselves, it would be a fallacious trap to pigeon-hole such organizations and their personnel.

The political economy of transition in Central and Eastern Europe is thus an enterprise that is as daring in practice and historically unprecedented, as it is an analytical laboratory subject to constant changes and open-minded reflection. The crumbling of the Berlin Wall almost a decade ago has opened unique opportunities for genuine intellectual inquiry, but also given rise to numerous dilemmas. It is this mixture of chances and constraints among more than 20 countries in Central and Eastern Europe, some of which did not exist in 1989/90, while others have only now returned to the political geography of the continent after more than four decades under the Soviet orbit, which makes this process so fascinating and confusing, so fragile at times, and yet equally sustainable. The *Lights at the End of the Tunnel* inform transition countries about thresholds they have crossed, all the while the final destination of their journeys and the respective arrival times have yet to be fully confirmed.

Meanwhile, the political economies of Central Europe proper - Hungary, Poland and the Czech Republic – are gradually moving out of the realm of Eastern Europe as such. The aforementioned three countries, alongside Slovenia and Estonia, can be expected to realign themselves over the next few years ahead of anticipated EU convergence plays. For this cluster of countries the issues are no longer whether a [new] government will turn back the clock on privatization or other basic structural reforms. Rather, it's whether these governments are up to the far more-challenging task of fine-tuning policies to keep their economies on track as the region's integration with the EU and the global economy grows. The region's late-stage reforms involve sticky tasks ranging from pension and health-care reforms to such relatively uncharted areas as battling short-term capital flows, like those that contributed to the Czech economic crisis in 1997, and the development of intermediate government structures that devolve economic decision-making closer to where the money is spent.

By contrast, second and third-tier countries such as Russia, Belarus, Ukraine, Romania, Slovakia and Bulgaria are struggling to attract investors, meeting EU standards of transformation in their respective political economies and consolidating the democratic processes. In other words, what is gradually emerging are manifest differences in the performance of political economies across Central and Eastern Europe, which gives rise to cleavages and the apprehension among lagging countries to be left behind in the region's transition processes. Put otherwise, in emerging economies of Central and Eastern Europe outside the EU, non-membership can thus reinforce divergence between the strong[er] and the weak[er], leaders and lagers, the ins and the outs.

The editor should like to acknowledge the support – intellectually and otherwise – from a variety of individuals and organizations. With a view to the latter, the initial idea for the book originates from a thought-provoking teaching experience at the *London School of Economics*. The post-graduate Master course *The Political Economy of Transition in Europe*, in which the editor engages in a variety of ways, has seen numerous highly talented students from East and West. Their intellectual insights and personal experiences in transition countries have allowed the editor to learn more than can be identified in these pages. It is a recognition of this talent that two so-called 'PETE-students' have been invited to publish their current reflections in the edited volume. Furthermore, the *DAAD*, the German Academic Exchange Service, gave the editor the unique professional opportunity to engage in the complexities of the *London School of Economics*. Among those that have made this volume come to fruition, knowingly or with their 'invisible insight', are: Claus Offe, Lukas Tsoukalis, Lutz Wingert and Karen Wördemann, Lord William Wallace of Saltaire, Lord Magnet Desay, as well as Péter Bod.

Finally, transition is not only a fascinating and challenging topic of inquiry. It is also an experience, a state of mind to which the editor has been subject during the past years. In the course of this journey, the editor has received illuminating and unconditional support from two individuals, which have repeatedly shown him the 'light(s) at the end of the tunnel'. It is to both of them that this volume is dedicated with love and gratitude.

Notes

1   Dedicated regional and global emerging-markets funds have targeted Central Europe ever since the early 1990s, when Budapest, Prague and Warsaw first set up stock markets and began opening their debt markets to foreigners. Initially, many investors viewed the region as a place for niche players with strong nerves. However, this perspective is starting to change. In April 1998, for instance, Polish government paper offered real yields on the order of 8 percent and a strengthening currency. Thus, to a growing number of portfolio investors, Central Europe is starting to look more like Portugal or Italy a decade ago: inflationary (although declining), relatively poor, but heading for better times amid a rise of EU accession-related inward investment.
2   This gradual change can also be illustrated with reference to the EBRD's operations. The share of portfolio loans and investments, which the EBRD is making towards Hungary, Poland, the Czech Republic, Estonia and Slovenia, has declined to 25 percent for the financial year 1997. By contrast, Russia's share of the total EBRD portfolio is currently 30 percent.

References

Dahrendorf, R. (1997), *After 1989. Morals, Revolution and Civil Society*, Macmillan Press: London.

IHT = *International Herald Tribune*, 18.04.1998, 'For Poland's Top Diplomat, an East-West Balance'.

Misztal, B.A. (1996), "Postcommunist Ambivalence: Becoming of a New Formation", in *European Journal of Sociology*, Vol. 37, No. 1, pp. 104-142.

2 The social and economic legacies of direct capital inflows: the case of Hungary

Péter Á. Bod

Direct investment flows: a slow start

Miracles do not happen easily in economics or politics, but surprises do. The Soviet Union collapsed sooner than ever anticipated. Poland, Hungary, Czechoslovakia and other nations in the region managed to restore parliamentary democracy, for the most part without violence, and started to recreate the market economy. The West was taken by surprise, too, but decided not to launch another *Marshall Plan*: capital markets would take care of the emerging economies. However, they did not. International banks took a cautious approach to the events of 1990, and with good reason: some of the new democracies were already financially bankrupt (Poland and Yugoslavia), while others were heavily indebted (Hungary and Bulgaria). FDI was generally expected to flow to sectors offering high returns due to shortage of capital, but direct capital flows were also to remain marginal for some time. This is not surprising. Yield is only one part of the *risk-yield equation,* and private capital market agents decided against investing in the former socialist countries immediately after such radical political changes: uncertainty and the lack of market institutions rendered investments too risky for mainstream institutions.

The *transformational recession* could be one of the explanatory factors for this slow start. Indeed, even the more developed Central-Eastern European (CEE) countries experienced an unexpectedly steep contraction in the first three years of transition. The cumulative loss of GDP in Poland amounted to 17.8 per cent in 1990-91, 18.3 per cent in Hungary, and slightly more in Czechoslovakia between 1989 and 1993 - a fall in output which, if official statistics are to be believed, was larger than that which occurred during the Great Depression of the 1930s (Rostowski 1996).

And yet another surprise: past reforms under socialism did not make much difference. Whatever reform had been introduced to a centrally planned economy, about a third of industrial output turned out to be useless as soon as the country stopped subsidising production and protecting its companies from foreign competition. With the benefit of hindsight one can see that "pure socialist production" - i.e. unfinished investments, unwanted stocks and other forms of "output for output's sake" - was lost in any case (Blejer and Coricelli 1995). Decades of experimentation with socialist market reforms did not save Yugoslavia, Poland or Hungary from the pain of adjustment after 1989, nor apparently did the lack of market socialism in Czechoslovakia aggravate the shock of transition. Irrespective of previous policies and variants of regime, these countries have all had to remove negative value added industries from their economies and re-capitalise state owned banks with negative share capital.

However, transformational recession, unlike depressions in established market economies, was not in itself a major obstacle to foreign investment (Hunya 1996). Some private capital did flow to certain transition countries, but not to others with similar depths of GDP contraction. *Hungary* represents a surprising *exception*. Annual capital inflows have totalled from 5 to 11 per cent of GDP since 1991. There have been years when the greater part of all FDI to the entire region, including Russia and Ukraine, has gone to the relatively small Hungarian economy. Therefore it is fair to say that private capital flows to the region, in the aggregate, have not lived up to expectations until very recently, but that some countries did manage to attract significant inflows.

Table 1
Flow of FDI into selected countries, 1989-96, US $ millions

	1991	1992	1993	1994	1995	1996	Aggregate
Bulgaria		42	55	105	82	100	425
Czech	511	983	517	1,024	2,720	1,264	7,120
Estonia		58	160	212	199	110	735
Hungary	1,459	1,471	2,339	1,097	4,410	1,986	13,260
Poland	117	284	580	542	1,134	2,741	5,398
Romania		77	94	347	404	210	1,186
Slovakia		100	156	178	134	177	623
Slovenia	41	113	112	131	170	180	743

Sources: *EBRD Transition Reports* (1995, 1997).

Other types of capital flow behaved somewhat differently, but did not change the overall picture. Apart from this, FDI is of particular significance for emerging economies: direct investments are regarded as crucial in transferring technological, marketing and management know-how to the host country. Joint ventures and fully foreign-controlled firms are expected to increase the economic competitiveness of the countries' international competitiveness as well as advance their access to world markets. Western academic advice and the encouragement of politicians since the onset of economic transition have certainly created expectations in the region that private funds and foreign market participants will help restore export growth and economic dynamism./

As we now know, the steep contraction of the early 1990s has not been followed by an equally steep take-off. Some countries did manage to grow faster than others, once the first phase of the transitional contraction was over, but the region as a whole has not reached its pre-transition level in terms of GDP per capita. Such a statement invites a closer look. What attracts investors to a particular transition country? Why Hungary? Have huge capital inflows delivered the promised transformational effect on the recipient country? Why are Hungarian growth rates remarkably lower than those of other countries in the region, despite Hungary's success with foreign investors?

These are important questions for the student of economic transition in general, and for anyone with a particular interest in the development of Hungary. Similar questions are also frequently raised by investment bank analysts. In the following text we shall look at three interconnected topics: (a) factors that drive the investment process; (b) the structure and nature of direct investments; and (c) the macro economic consequences of direct capital inflows. In this paper I shall not restrict myself to analysis of relevant data, but shall also offer some examples from my own personal experience as a former Cabinet member who was involved in policy-making for both domestic and foreign investment (e.g. the tax code, investment incentives, etc.), and who conducted negotiations with foreign investors. These observations from my personal recollection are distinguished from the main text by inclusion in italicised boxes.

Opportunities offered and risks perceived

International capital flows may take many forms including bank loans, equity investments into existing companies, and green field investments. Money is fungible, and one form of funding can easily be transformed into another, thus rendering the distinction of various kinds of moneys a relative, if not a futile matter. However, from the viewpoint of transition countries *direct investment* stands out as perhaps the most welcome form of capital inflow. This is because FDI is seen to involve a particular *mix*: funds plus the potential of technological, marketing and/or management transfer. As we shall see, this potential does not always materialise, and even if it does, its diffusion takes time.

The initial conditions for the transformation of the CEE region were unique. As distinct from genuinely developing countries, the economies concerned had become fairly diversified, populated by a limited number of industrial and trading (state-owned) firms which were manned by a relatively well-educated, if under motivated labour force. After decades of high saving and investment rates, there was no general shortage of physical assets. However, as soon as the first governments had removed state subsidies and restrictions to competition, most of these assets quickly proved to be in the wrong place and were typically severely obsolete. Under these conditions, foreign capital did not find it easy to enter the region. The end of the virtual inaccessibility of the region's economies certainly offered a variety of business opportunities from sales of consumer goods to loans for under funded state-owned or new private firms; from participating in privatization to establishing joint ventures or investing in the "green field". But here enters the *risk factor* which has rarely been addressed in literature on the topic.

Medium- and long-term bank lending is sensitive to the overall risk level that is the sum of *sovereign risk* and *counterpart risk*. In the earliest years of transition only a few countries possessed ratings from the major credit rating institutions. In fact, in 1989 Hungary was the only country with a credit rating. With the exception of the Czech Republic "investment grade" ratings were not granted until the sixth year of transition. Thus, sovereign risk was regarded as fairly high; on top of which were added the risks of doing business with local banks and firms. The risk-mitigating institutions of a fully-fledged market economy, such as financial and legal services, accounting firms, dispute settlement fora, goods and currency exchanges, etc. were still largely non-existent.

Not only banks were sensitive to the perceived risks and the lack of a legal and financial framework. Portfolio investments are best executed through reliable capital market institutions, first and foremost a transparent stock exchange. It was therefore important that the Budapest Stock Exchange was re-created in 1990 after four decades. But for any *Bourse* to gain acceptance and become capable of absorbing serious money it will take a while to achieve. Decisions on direct investments are less strongly influenced by sovereign risk or the relative maturity of the domestic capital market. What investors need in the first place is close knowledge of the local firms and factor/product markets. The process through which strategic investors identify sectors and locations of interest is time-consuming; they usually conduct detailed discussion with central and local authorities before committing themselves.

Such are the considerations from the investors side. On the other hand, those of us who were making decisions on behalf of the host country faced different priorities and constraints. As well as needing fresh capital, countries with high inherited debts (such as Hungary) also had to find refinancing - at almost any price. Privatization offers a foreign-currency-earning instrument. However, saleable assets were few in the very first years of transformation, and their sale value was extremely uncertain. Former "star companies" had generally lost their *Comecon* markets and were standing idle. State monopolies (gas, oil, and electricity) were still functioning under an inadequately defined legal and regulatory framework. Problem companies and those requiring financial and technological reorganization could not offer promising business deals. The companies' capacity to bear debt was invariably limited, whether state-owned or private. The former faced an uncertain future while waiting to be privatized, and the latter were unable to provide a proven track record or offer collateral to banks.

Economies with no sizeable debt were not under this sort of refinancing pressure, either as a result of former orthodox financial policies (e.g. Czechoslovakia under Husak), or due to forced repayment of debts (e.g. Ceausescu's Romania). The Romanian method proved shockingly expensive in terms of human suffering and economic cost; Czechoslovak financial orthodoxy, for that matter, was accompanied by orthodox communist policies and self-imposed near-isolation from the world economy. Whatever their background, when profound transformation began, these countries lacked the required capital market institutions and established channels of capital inflows, and all represented a degree of financial and commercial risk which was too great for private sector participants at the time. In short, most former socialist economies were characterised by a *limited capacity to absorb capital* in the early phase of transition.

Overcoming reluctance and inertia requires *policy actions*. The three most comparable countries - Poland, Hungary and Czechoslovakia applied similar, as well as different approaches. Similarities characterise their legal regulations: in all these countries 100 per cent foreign ownership, repatriation of profits and dividends, and provision of full current account and near-full capital account currency convertibility were part of the incentives offered after 1990. Poland and Hungary also provided generous tax breaks, while Czechoslovakia declared that foreign and local investors were to be taxed on equal terms. In reality, the government made sure of retaining some leeway to allow it to woo big investors, thus the trade policy incentives provided for the Volkswagen – Skoda deal in 1991/92.

The main differences in approach to foreign investors manifest themselves in *privatization policy* or in the consequences of this policy. All governments applied a set of instruments for transferring state assets into the private sector; thus each individual privatization practice in the region is a *mix of methods*, ranging from free transfer of state property to local authorities and the social security fund to sale of assets through competitive tenders. There are, however, marked differences in the composition of that mix. The Czechoslovak government - and later the Czech Republic - favoured the equal-access voucher scheme, while in Poland management buy-outs and sales through investment funds emerged as the main method. Hungary's characteristic approach was through sale to outside owners (see Table 2).

Table 2

Methods of privatization for medium-sized and large enterprises in transition economies (% of total)

Country	Sale to outside owners	Voucher	Buyout	Restitution	Other	Still in State hands
Czech Rep						
by number	32	22	0	9	28	10
by value	5	50	0	2	3	40
Hungary						
by number	38	0	7	0	33	22
by value	40	0	2	4	12	42
Poland						
by number	3	6	14	0	23	54

Source: World Bank (1996). Data are end of 1995.

Privatization techniques relate to FDI both directly and indirectly. In countries where foreigners are offered the opportunity to participate in privatization, the climate appears conducive to FDI inflows. This policy attitude is the direct link between privatization and capital investments.

As the case of Hungarian privatization proves, the market sale of assets automatically favours foreign buyers over domestic buyers, who can hardly compete with them in terms of purchasing power. Few local actors were capable of entering an open tender or offering the highest cash bid. Thus, in the first full year of Hungarian privatization about 80 per cent of revenues accrued to the *Privatization Agency* through the sale of state assets oroginated from foreigners. Hungary also emerged as the only country of the region with significant foreign direct investment in 1991, in spite of contraction of output, which was nearly as deep as in other transition countries. Whether these noteworthy figures of inflows are a sign of success in attracting foreign capital, or an indication of the weaknesses in creating a new entrepreneurial stratum depends on one's point of view. In fact, the government of Prime Minister *József Antall* (1990-93) made great efforts to form the appropriate legal and financial conditions for local businesses, and managed to balance the foreign/domestic composition by the end of its term in office.

It is worth emphasising that, in spite of corrective measures, the nature of direct sales gives rise to a predominance of foreign buyers. The consequences of the open door policy also make the transformation of the economy more radical, although in the Hungarian case micro-shocks went mostly unnoticed as they took place within the privatized firms, without much ado. The pattern as demonstrated in the Hungarian privatization is as follows. First, outside buyers (mostly foreign) quickly transform corporate governance by introducing their own management system. Having invested hard cash, the new owners will then radically upgrade formerly state-owned companies by reducing redundant labour and closing down non-core activities. Reorganization generally involves further investment into both machinery and facilities, as well as financial restructuring through loans from parent companies. It has to be added here for the sake of cross-national comparisons that in Hungarian national statistics, both the original sale and the subsequent capital increase or reorganization-related investments will be registered as FDI flows.

Hungary may be the country where sale to outside owners is most prevalent, but this technique was applied in other countries too, such as the high profile cases in the Czech Republic (SPT Telecom,

Volkswagen-Skoda, Philip Morris-Tabak, Continental-Barum, Sass 1997). In the case of Poland, sales to foreigners have mostly been limited, but capital increases in already privatized companies are becoming more frequent. Lack of sizeable direct investments during the early years may be ascribed to the then unresolved rescheduling negotiations being conducted between the Paris and London clubs and the Polish government. Direct investors are not as sensitive to country risk as banks and investment funds, but the macro economic uncertainty associated with indebtedness must have been a restraining factor for larger potential investors.

There is also an indirect link between a country's attitude to foreign ownership and the amount of FDI and privatization revenues. Perhaps it is best to limit the argument to Hungary, the country with which the author is most familiar. The first democratically elected government came into office in the middle of a foreign debt crisis, which had elicited a pro-foreign capital bias even under the outgoing reform-communist government. In its final days, the outgoing government was forced to turn to the IMF and to liberalise the economy. This is how the two-tier banking system came to be introduced and foreign investments were legalised in 1987-88. These new opportunities did not result in massive inflows before the change of regime, but some investments did take place, such as in the lighting industry.

The first major privatization transaction took place under transitional circumstances and partly by default. The lighting products and equipment manufacturer *Tungsram*, one of the flagships of Hungarian industry, had become irreparably indebted to a (newly created, state-owned) Hungarian commercial bank. Since the bank (MHB) had been set up the previous year, undercapitalized, and thus unable to provide additional financing, its management decided to swap loans for equity and then sell it. The only foreign buyer to volunteer was an Austrian bank, which quickly resold its equity in *Tungsram* to *General Electric* (GE) at a profit. This deal cast light on the lack of professionalism of the newly established Hungarian banks, but was also the first case of privatization (albeit in a roundabout way). This took place in 1989, before the change of regime. GE has gradually reduced the number of staff to less than half its original level, and drastically cut

21

down the once famous local R&D staff. Later on, production and export started to grow, and Budapest-based R&D activities began to recover, once the new owner had realised how cost-effective it was to locate research in Hungary, where pay is relatively low and academic standards are high.

The democratically elected new government of 1990 was committed to introducing a fully-fledged market economy and also vowed to keep up the debt repayments in order to maintain the country's external creditworthiness. This policy option involved providing all the incentives necessary to attract foreign investment; in fact there was not much choice left as big investors kept referring to sweeteners that had been offered to others. This is the case with another major American corporation that appeared on the scene during the transitional months. Through its German subsidiary *Opel*, General Motors searched for sites to build a new engine plant and finally selected one of the plants of *RÁBA*, a truck producer based in Györ, western Hungary. The GM (Opel) deal was concluded with the outgoing Communist government which, considering it vital to secure the transaction, was willing to offer numerous incentives and prerogatives to the investor. To date, this original investment has resulted in capital inflows of about US $0.5 billion, and has certainly increased the interest of other multinationals in expanding their activity into Hungary.

Soon after the GM deal was struck in early 1990, weeks before the general elections, *Ford Motor Co.* sent a team to Hungary to study opportunities and talk to the government. The Ford delegation paid the author a surprise visit in my little room at the research institute. They wanted to talk to me as an advisor to the opposition and as an economist about their plan to build a plant somewhere in Hungary to produce two particular vehicle components. Although eastern Hungary was badly in need of new investment, they made it clear that a first-rate infrastructure (i.e. a motorway and an airport nearby) was essential. Ford eventually selected *Székesfehérvár*, a city to the west of Budapest, and since then has invested well over US $ 100 million. Some months after that first informal visit, as Minister for Industry and Trade, I conducted negotiations with Ford managers who fought determinedly for extra incentives - above those offered by the investment law - similar to those granted to GM. I personally have found American executives the most eager of all investors to obtain government grants and tariff protection.

The example of the *Suzuki* plant illustrates another approach to investment. This family-owned business came to Hungary in 1990-91 partly to export, but equally importantly to sell. Unlike the American automotive investors, Mr. Suzuki insisted on building the plant in a place where there had never been any socialist industry, confessing that he needed "farmers and housewives, rather than spoilt workers" for his plant. The other difference was his willingness to run at a loss for a couple of years (as the plant would be below the optimal size for a full car assembly) before he felt confident enough to change from one-shift (!) to two- and later three-shift mode.

The car industry has been the single most important investor in the region. *Volkswagen* has invested in all four "Visegrad" countries; *GM-Opel* in Poland and Hungary; *Fiat* and *Daewoo* in Poland; *Suzuki, Ford*, and *United Technologies* in Hungary (Simonian 1997). Car manufacturers typically invest into the "greenfield", although not exclusively: German firms do, albeit reluctantly, invest in and then upgrade existing firms, e.g. *Skoda*. Car manufacturers may be more willing to cross borders in their search for appropriate production locations, but other industries also testify to the link between direct investment activities and a country's general attitude to privatization. After eight years it is easy to detect a pattern: all the factors, both legal and cultural, that facilitate privatization by direct sale also make 'greenfield' and 'brown field' investments easier. The presence of well-known firms from one particular country may influence others - often their *competitors* - to include the target country in their development plans. This may be regarded as a *herd instinct*, but there is more to it than that: the emergence of a *cluster* of related firms may provide increasing returns to scale, as the "new trade theory" (Krugman 1997) has noticed, and also helps reduce the perceived risks associated with coming to and producing in the target country.

This is how combined privatization revenues and direct investment transfers reached US $ 1.5 billion in Hungary in 1991. These inflows have been instrumental in maintaining the solvency of the country, and accelerating the structural changes in Hungarian corporate governance. However, these amounts proved insufficient to impress rating agencies:

Hungary only regained its 'investment grade' sovereign rating at the end of 1996. This discrepancy between the judgement of industrialist and debt rating agencies has been with us for years - an interesting phenomenon of international business. The level of trust of the industrial business community does not have to accord with the verdict of financial analysts.

Origin, structure and types of direct investment in Hungary

Hungary's direct-sale-dominated privatization practice should not be regarded as the skilful execution of a grand strategy. The new government of Prime Minister József Antall had partly to delay, and partly to give up its original plans to support the emergence of a new middle class of Hungarian entrepreneurs, and was forced by circumstances to sell a greater part of the available state assets to cash-rich buyers, i.e. to foreigners, than originally intended. The government was also urged to offer some incentives to multinationals, which were not available to local businesses. Some of the consequences of this process later proved problematic for the budget, employment and trade. On the other hand, Hungary managed to attract clusters of international businesses during the critical early years of transition. These years were, in a certain sense, exceptional for the entire region: *Poland* was still in debt negotiations, *Yugoslavia* was to disintegrate, *Czechoslovakia* was to separate, and steep contraction was occurring all over the region. One may assume that Hungary's early successes in attracting foreign capital were only due to a lack of opportunities in neighbouring countries. It is therefore useful to look closely at the period that followed.

Most economies of the region - though not yet in the *former Soviet Union* or the *Balkans* - reached the trough in 1993. Investments started to grow, privatization went ahead and new sectors were opened up for foreign investors (e.g. banking, utilities). Net FDI flows to the region further increased from a meagre US $ 4.2 bn in 1992 to US $ 12.2 bn in 1995 (EBRD 1995). Inflows to Hungary remained high in 1992 and particularly in 1993, which turned out to be a strong year when the annual volume of FDI flows was topped up by a huge privatization deal

24

between the Hungarian state and a consortium formed by *Deutsche Telekom* and *Ameritech* (Bod 1997). Besides German and US investment, there was also strong interest from *Dutch, French* and *Belgian* investors.

In Hungary the year 1994 does not fit the trend: foreign inflows represented less than half the level of the previous year, and even less than in 1991, the year of sharp contraction. The key is politics: there was an election in May 1994, after which the incoming Socialist government practically stopped initiating any new privatization transactions for several months. Taking the CEE region as a whole, Hungary's share of cumulative FDI inflows is still about two-fifths - a remarkable achievement for a country of limited market size. It is true that Hungary after 1994 opened up those sectors to (foreign) investors which are not generally the first on the list of government priorities elsewhere since they involve selling *domestic markets* to external buyers: banking, insurance, and water, gas and power utilities. It is logical to ask whether the high and increasing share of some countries in capital flows to Hungary will not lead to a foreign presence strong enough to be regarded as *dependence*. The Antall Government certainly gave consideration to this issue, and regarded a fairly wide distribution among various countries of origin as advantageous.

Table 3
FDI in Hungary by country of origin, share of total in percent

May-93	%	Dec-94	%	Dec-95	%	Dec-96	%
1. USA	29.0	USA	27.0	Germany	29.0	Germany	28.0
2. Germany	19.5	Germany	24.5	USA	24.0	USA	26.0
3. Austria	13.5	Austria	13.4	Austria	10.5	Austria	10.5
4. France	7.0	France	6.8	France	9.0	France	10.0
5. Italy	6.5	Italy	5.0	Italy	4.0	Holland	4.5
6. Japan	4.5	UK	5.0	Holland	4.0	Italy	4.0

Source: *PK (1997).*

In some countries the pre-eminence of Germany as the single biggest investor has been unquestionable since the early days of the transition period, for example in the Czech Republic, Slovakia and Croatia (East-West Investment News 1995/1996). The amounts of German investment have been growing throughout the period, particularly in the CEE countries nearest to Germany. The composition of the *origin of capital* indicates that Hungary has been able to attract investors from many major countries. It is important for any capital-importing country not to be over-dependent on one particular economy or region. As mentioned earlier, there was a tacit government policy to maintain, if possible, a diversified distribution among investor nations.

This policy was not oriented against particular countries, and did not contradict other objectives such as transparency, fairness and application of international "best practice": it was applied as an additional feature of privatization/investment policy. As an example of geo-political considerations, one may mention the government's active diplomacy in France, Italy and some smaller non-traditional investor countries in the early 1990s, which was aimed at intensifying investor interest in Hungary. This diversification of sources of capital was sustained until 1995, when, as we shall see, major shifts took place in the privatization process.

Detailed statistics produced recently by the Hungarian Statistical Office (1996) show not only the comparative value of FDI by country of origin (as measured by statutory capital stakes in joint ventures), but also the sectoral composition of FDI. The true value of this publication lies in the detail: from it one can draw conclusions about the sectoral, regional, and size structure of firms with foreign ownership in Hungary. Data on the *sectoral composition* of FDI in 1993-94 indicate that the most important investor countries were represented in all major branches of the economy. Some single large-scale transactions such as the privatization of Hungarian telecommunications giant *MATÁV* in 1993 may distort the general picture by momentarily inflating one country's share in a particular branch (e.g. Germany's and the US's shares in telecommunications and transport in 1993).

Table 4
FDI in Hungary by sector and country of origin (%, 1993-94)

Origin/Sector	Total		German		USA		Austria		Holland		UK	
	93	94	93	94	93	94	93	94	93	94	93	94
Food, tobacco, beverages	17	17	10	11	11	11	3	13	41	52	28	18
Chemicals	5	7	4	7	11	4	5	9	5	4	10	11
Machinery, equipment	14	15	5	12	30	32	11	9	0	1	1	4
Trade	8	12	8	12	7	9	12	13	12	11	22	27
Construction	3	5	2	4	0	4	10	10	0	0	0	8
Finance	9	10	7	8	3	4	13	12	25	19	1	6
Real estate	4	6	2	6	6	9	8	8	8	4	2	2
Transport, Telecoms	22	9	46	20	31	7	2	3	0	4	9	3
Other sectors	6	6	4	3	2	9	10	8	7	3	6	12
Total	100	100	100	100	100	100	100	100	100	100	100	100

Source: *Hungarian Central Statistical Office (1996).*

Individual sectors, e.g. trade or chemicals may be too aggregate a statistical measure to illustrate the role of specific investments in the host country, yet the comparison of the sectoral composition of FDI and the sectoral composition of the host country does offer the opportunity to draw some qualitative conclusions regarding their congruence, that is whether the structure of foreign investments harmonises with the production and investment structures of the host country. Even without a formal statistical test of congruence, it is easy to see that the sectoral composition of German, Austrian and US investments reflect the overall sectoral structure of the Hungarian economy. This is especially striking compared to the structure of Japanese, Dutch or Belgian investments which are concentrated in two or three sectors. One can venture to state that *the more equal the sectoral* (and regional, for that matter) *distribution of capital inflows, the more likely it is that FDI is organically linked to the structure of the host economy.*

In the Hungarian case there is no sign of a "colonial" pattern, that is, foreign investments concentrated in a few primary sectors. These data rather provide some evidence for '*Kojima-type*' FDI[1]: large scale US and Japanese investments are concentrated in manufacturing sectors (the automotive industry) with the aim of exporting the end products from Hungary. Table 4 (page 27) reflects the situation in 1993-94. Since then, further privatization and FDI inflows have somewhat altered the picture. Foreign participation has become pronounced in banking and insurance, and high in certain infra structural branches (telecoms, water and power), construction and the food industry. Given that the factor most strongly affecting the distribution of FDI is the privatization process, it is important to distinguish the sub-categories of FDI, that is (i) privatization; (ii) new ('greenfield') investments; and (iii) portfolio investments.

1   Participation in *privatization* by external investors requires a fairly thorough knowledge of the country and the particular firm on sale. Cultural and geographic proximity helps: data show that the leading position of Germany in *privatization* is more pronounced than in overall FDI. German (and Austrian) firms tend to be more willing to acquire equity in existing state-owned firms than investors from countries less familiar with the region. This willingness is partly cultural on the investor's side. There is also a parallel factor on the host country's side: the willingness of state-owned enterprise managers and privatization agencies to propose transactions to Central European clients is formed by experience and expectations.

   Privatization involving foreigners tends to be more politically sensitive than green field investments; it may be regarded as 'foreigners buying up our national assets'. It is also worth mentioning that the number of Hungarian firms to have been acquired in the privatization process by German, and Austrian or French investors is rather high, and the average size of privatization deals is relatively low, indicating a more general, economy-wide interest compared to some other investor nations. Japan's absence from the privatization process, for instance, is conspicuous. There is however no Anglo-Saxon aversion to buying up former state assets: the share of the US or UK in privatization was, until 1995, similar to or higher than their average share in overall Hungarian FDI. Significant changes in the foreign configuration of Hungarian privatization took place after the somewhat hastily executed year-end sale of 1995. Compared to the situation as of April 1994, the shares of *Germany* and *France* in Hungarian privatization increased significantly at the cost of former large players such as the *US, Austria* and the *UK*.

2   Privatization is only one route to acquiring a stake in an economy, the other avenue being *new direct investment*. Not surprisingly, in this respect it is the US that leads in Hungary, as in most other countries of the region. The US lead may be partly explained by the commercial and technological success of GE's and GM's earlier operations. GM's positive impressions must have sent a strong signal to other car producers: as we have seen, *Ford* and *Suzuki* also acted quickly, and in 1993 *Audi* selected Győr (western Hungary) as the site for its new engine plant.

The Audi deal was a great diplomatic success for the Hungarian economy: Audi had investigated over 100 potential sites and Győr eventually won over Magdeburg (Eastern Germany) in spite of some attempts at moral persuasion on the German government's part. The plant is a high-tech facility where labour costs do not count for much; what matters most is workplace culture and reliability. Size of the country or extra incentives played no part. According to a recent press report, Audi Hungaria will launch assembly of the TT Coupé model (20,000 per year) and later the TT Roadster (10,000 per year) in 1998, and the engine plant will also turn out new V8 engines. This plant will thus become the largest single investor in Hungary. There are indications that Audi's presence invited further industrial investors in related sectors (such as metallurgy and car parts). *VAW Aluminium AG* (Germany) recently opened a new DM 80 million cylinder head plant to supply new aluminium engine block units on orders from Audi and Mercedes.

Table 5
Green field FDI in Hungary 1996 (US $ millions)

No.	Company	Investment	Factual	Description
1	General Motors (USA)	500		Car and engines
2	Audi (Germany)	400	250	Car and engines
3	Suzuki (Japan)	250		Car assembly
4	IBM (USA)	135	25	Electronics: parts
5	Ford (USA)	135	25	Automotive: parts
6	Guardian Glass (US)	110		Glass
7	Philips (Netherlands)	100	15	Electronics
8	Fuchs Metallwerke (FRG)	75		Metals
9	Coca Cola (USA)	70		Beverages
10	VAW Alum. (Germany)	60		Metals
11	Tetra Pack (Sweden)	55		Packaging
12	Schollers (Germany)	50		Foodstuffs
13	K. Nordenia (Germany)	50		Synthetic Fibres
14	Pharmavit	50		Pharmaceuticals
15	Columbian Chem. (USA)	40		Synthetic Rubber
16	Stollwerck (Germany)	40		Confectionery
17	ITT Automotive (Germany)	30	5	Automotive: parts
18	Rondo (Austria)	25		Packaging
19	Aga (Sweden)	20		Gas industry
20	Ada (Germany)	20		Furniture

Source: *Diczházi (1997).*

3   As for *portfolio investments*, current statistics are not reliable enough to trace the country of origin. However, it seems logical to say that capital inflows of a short-term nature, and with no intention to take a controlling part in corporate governance, are

less influenced by geographical and cultural-historical proximity. The players in this business are mainly investment funds, banks and financial houses of a *multinational* nature. In contrast to privatization and certain large-scale industrial projects, portfolio investments in Hungary had rather a late start. One reason might have been the country's initial risk rating ('speculative grade'), the other is the limited size of the stock exchange. The direct sale policy of the Hungarian privatization method indirectly led to the most promising firms being sold to strategic investors rather than through the stock exchange. Some national blue chips have, however, been introduced to the *Bourse* (e.g. oil monopoly *MOL*, or the national savings bank *OTP*), and some foreign investors have taken advantage of the fast-growing Budapest exchange.

Whatever the type of foreign flow, its composition and volume tend to change over time. There may be shifts in government policy, such as changes in the approach to privatization. The Socialist-Free Democrat administration that came to power in Budapest in summer 1994 first attempted to favour friendly investors and the management class, where their supporters predominated, by stopping the sale of state assets through open tender, introducing 'quick' and 'simplified' privatization methods instead. By now it has become evident that all-quick and simplified methods open up wide avenues for corruption and favouritism.

This shift in privatization policy coincided with a deterioration in the country's credit ratings at the end of 1994. In March 1995 the Socialist-Free Democrat coalition was obliged to introduce measures which included re-launching privatization. In a rapidly deteriorating investment climate, the privatization agencies were bound to sell state assets at any price and as quickly as possible, regardless of the market or country of origin. The sale of natural monopolies and major banks to foreigners resulted in sizeable hard currency revenues in December 1995, and thus contributed to a drop in the amount of external debt and in debt ratios. The capital flight, which took place before and after the 1994 elections, was reversed in 1995 with the re-launch of privatization, devaluation of the currency and the introduction of a pre-announced crawling peg rate for the *forint*. The crawling peg reduced the level of uncertainty over exchange rate volatility. However, the new exchange rate mechanism eliminated the exchange risk not only for the export sectors, but also for the holders of "hot" money as well - short terms inflows started to pour in to take advantage of the risk-free interest differentials. Eventually such inflows, whatever the motivation behind them, helped finance the trade deficit and improve Hungary's foreign debt ratio. The macro economic burden of the inherited debt did not go away, but the shadow of heavy indebtedness did.

It is now clear for the CEE countries that improved sovereign credit ratings and successful conclusion of privatization have been changing the pattern of capital flows, including direct investments. Import substitution and capture of specific rent-creating market anomalies as motives to invest in transition countries tend to diminish. FDI will increasingly be driven by motives of efficiency, associated with the globalization of production, trade and finance. Cultural factors and geography will still count, but as time goes by their significance is likely to decrease.

Where are the dividends?

Strong capital inflows into manufacturing, infrastructure and banking should be reflected in increased international competitiveness and productivity. Hungary has recorded the highest proportion of FDI of all the CEE countries, and so it is appropriate to ask whether this distinctive feature of the country's development has resulted in the expected benefits. Studies on the link between direct investments in productive sectors and industrial restructuring explore the resulting change of export structure (Statistical Service 1997). It is expected that the higher the share of FDI in capital stock/employment/GDP of a given country, the faster the export structure will improve. Improvement in the former socialist economies is supposed to materialise in a decrease in energy-intensive and (cheap) labour-intensive sectors such as steel and raw materials, textiles and clothing, respectively, and an increase in the machinery, transport and other equipment sectors. As expected, all three leading CEE countries managed to upgrade their export structure during the first five years of transformation, particularly as compared to less successful transition countries (e.g. Romania, see table 6 below).

Table 6
Share of machinery and transport equipment in export to the EU

	Czech Rep.		Hungary		Poland		Romania	
	1990	*1994*	*1990*	*1994*	*1990*	*1994*	*1990*	*1994*
share (%)	21	31	20	36	16	21	11	11

Source: *Hunya (1997).*

According to this data, the most favourable structural changes are evident in the case of Hungary and the Czech Republic, while Polish exports to the EU are dominated by a high share of labour-intensive light industry products. It is plausible to link these changes to differences not only in industrial traditions but also in FDI flows and privatization patterns. Poland's low share of FDI and slow privatization to outsiders must be relevant, in that Polish firms have typically integrated with EU partners through co-operation and outward processing agreements. At the same time, in the Czech Republic, and especially in Hungary, a high and growing share of the economy has been integrated into the world economy through multinational and/or transnational companies. According to the latest available figures (first half of 1997), 44 per cent of all Hungarian export trade comes from product group STIC-7, i.e. machinery, electric and electronic products and parts, and transport equipment including motor industry - a significant change in just a single year (the figure for the first half of 1996 was 37 per cent, see Statistical Service 1997).

Another indicator of the depth of restructuring is productivity. A recent UN ECE survey reveals a lesser-known aspect of transformation which sets Poland and Hungary aside from the Czech (and for that matter the Slovak) case. While in the former Czechoslovakia and later in the Czech Republic the first years of transition were characterised by a deep decline in labour productivity, particularly in industry, Poland and Hungary, the latter often labelled 'gradualist', experienced fast recovery and a steep increase in productivity. As measures of labour productivity relate output to labour employed, Poland's impressive high productivity figures for 1992 to 1994 are easy to explain in view of the strong growth of Polish output since 1992. What is rather surprising is that the Czech so-called 'shock therapy' was so greatly muted by the deep decline in productivity, which reveals that employment in industry and elsewhere did not shrink much, while output contracted drastically. Observers may also find it surprising that Hungarian labour productivity in general, and in industry in particular, grew so rapidly during 1993 through 1995 - much faster than the rate of GDP. This is indicative of far-reaching structural change in the corporate sector (EBRD 1996).

Reviewing Hungarian privatization practice and the growing role of foreign direct investors, one can see the link between these policy variables and the productivity figures. It is enough to refer to what happened in the newly emerging automotive industry, or other sectors dominated by foreigners. The medium- and large- scale foreign investors have created about 40,000 new jobs in industry, but backward and forward linkages with Hungarian subcontractors are rare for the time being (PK 1997). Privatizations and industrial reorganizations, whether involving foreign or Hungarian owners, have greatly reduced the head-count. There is not much difference between locally and foreign-owned businesses as far as the modalities of corporate reorganization are concerned, except in one respect: links with former suppliers. While locally privatized firms tend to retain at least some of their former business partners, foreign ownership - which frequently means foreign management - in most cases leads to the termination of former supply contracts.

This fact casts light on an unexpected feature of Hungarian development: in spite of the above-mentioned structural changes, the trade balance has been systematically negative in recent years. Observers are surprised to find that fully or partly foreign-owned (FO) firms as a sector have added far more to national imports than to overall export, while the sector consisting of locally owned (LO) firms showed a trade surplus in 1991 and 1992, and since then has run a smaller trade deficit than FO firms.

Table 7
Contribution of foreign- (FO) and locally owned (LO) firms
to trade in Hungary (US $ billions)

	1992	1993	1994	1995	1996
FO import	4.1	5.6	8.4	9.7	10-11.0
FO export	3.5	3.9	5.8	7.5	8-9.0
Trade balance	-0.6	-1.7	-2.5	-2.2	-2.5
LO import	6.0	5.7	2.9	5.7	N/A
LO export	6.6	4.2	1.8	5.4	N/A
Trade balance	0.6	-1.5	-1.1	-0.3	N/A
All import	10.0	11.3	11.2	15.3	16.8
All export	10.0	8.1	7.6	12.8	14.2
Trade balance	0.0	-3.2	-3.7	-2.4	-2.6
FO share of trade balance	N/A	53 %	70 %	92 %	97 %

Source: *PK (1997).*

These figures should be handled with care. Unfortunately, the once reputable Hungarian statistical service has become notoriously slow and unreliable. Vital data are delayed or subject to serious amendment later. It is still not clear whether the 1993-94 deterioration of trade and balance of payments was mainly due to premature consumption growth - as the incoming Socialist-Free Democrat coalition claimed, citing indicators of loss of competitiveness and a disproportionate growth of wages - or mostly the result of an investment boom in infrastructure and industry.

Even the size of the trade balance has been cast in doubt. Recent official data include the export/import figures for so-called duty-free zones: most of the above-mentioned large joint ventures or fully foreign-owned firms registered at least part of their activity in these zones. Recent official publications reveal that industrial duty-free zones are responsible for US $ 2.1 bn of export and US $ 1.6 bn of import in the first six months of 1997 alone, thus improving the trade balance by US $ 0.5 bn. One can only wonder whether the 1993 decline of Hungarian export was real, or whether the decline registered by the statistical office covered nothing but visible LO and FO trade, ignoring the dynamic duty-free sector. The pre-1995 trade figures are admittedly not comparable to current data. The recent inclusion of duty-free trade turnover in published statistics makes it appear as if there has been a dramatic upswing, while distorting the impression given by the 1992-94 figures.

It is also probable that leads and lags play a bigger role in such a small economy than is generally recognised. It is enough to make one big investment with a hundred million US-dollars' worth of imported equipment to push up import statistics, or to register as an import some large-scale shipment from Russia under the settlement of previous Soviet-era claims by the Hungarian state. Capital flight is another variable that can cause confusion to observers. But whatever methodological weaknesses we may find here, the conclusion is that up until now the *large foreign owned sector has added at least as much to the import intensity as it will ultimately to the export intensity of the Hungarian economy.* It will take some time - between one and three years - before major foreign direct investments enter their full productive phase and start to improve the macro economic picture. An increase in import intensity and transitional unemployment, as well as a temporary loss of state revenues; one may regard these outcomes as a small price to pay for the modernising effect of strong capital inflows into Hungary. There are, however, other worrying aspects: FDI tends to follow a strong *regional pattern.* The pattern is fairly consistent: most of the direct investments take place either in the capital or on the Vienna-Budapest corridor. Therefore the long-awaited modernising effect has so far been limited to the more developed areas of Hungary.

Table 8
Regional distribution of FDI (in percent of total)

	May 1993	December 1994	December 1995	December 1996
Budapest and Pesty	51	49	46	46
North Transdanubia	25	27	28	26
Central Hungary	13	12	13	12
North-east Hungary	6	7	7	10
South Transdanubia	5	5	6	6

Source: *Diczházi (1997).*

Not that one can blame foreign investors for locating their plants in the country's more developed areas, closer to the western borders, and thus more accessible. This pattern is logical, but at the same time it is indicative of the governments' inability to create proper business conditions elsewhere in the country. FDI-flows express the foreign investors' preferences, but these are practically identical with those of local businesses who also want better roads, telephone services and public education, as well as households with adequate purchasing power. A quick comparison of production and investment data, household savings or any other indicator of the economic activity of the Hungarian counties would result in a very similar geographical pattern to that shown in table 8 above.

This leads us to an aspect, which this contribution cannot ignore: the *state of the non-FDI-related business sector.* This covers, of course, the greater part of the economy. With the accelerating expansion of the FDI sector, modest growth of the overall economy (1 to 3 per cent increase of GDP annually in the last three years) can only take place arithmetically if the locally owned part of the Hungarian economy does not grow, or only grows at a snail's pace. If, for example, we look at industrial activity from another viewpoint, i.e. in terms of *size* of business, we find that in the first half of 1997 - which will be the first genuine growth year since 1994 - large firms (employing over 300) grew much faster than average, while medium-sized firms (employing 50 to 300) grew slower than average. The output of smaller firms has been decreasing (KSH 1997). In the Hungarian case there is a strong link between *size* and *ownership*. Locally owned businesses tend to be smaller, and foreign-owned businesses are over-represented among larger firms. And the larger, mostly multinational firms, which often operate in duty-free zones, have shown an impressive growth rate: exports from these industrial zones increased by over 50 per cent in the first six months of 1997 compared to the year before, while imports rose by 35 per cent (KSH 1997). Here again it is not the dynamism of the sector benefiting from foreign capital that begs explanation, but the below-national-average vitality of other sectors and regions.

Local SMEs have partly themselves to blame for this neglect. It has become standard practice in Hungary to under-report size of activity, number of employees and size of profits in order to avoid tax and extremely high social security contributions. Hungarian entrepreneurs, on average, tend to declare net income below the wage level of the average employee working for the median entrepreneur - a farce in itself, tolerated by an impotent state. On the other hand, these tactics backfire when the same entrepreneur applies for a bank loan to expand his business, and learns that such a small and only marginally profitable venture doesn't even exist as far as a professionally managed financial institution is concerned. This is a vicious circle, which should be broken by reducing the level of taxes and other such levies, and by strengthening tax collection. But why are taxes and social security revenues so high in the first place?

This is perhaps the key factor in the Hungarian case. Ever since the onset of the change of regime the entire privatization strategy and a whole series of economic policy measures have been influenced by the burden of foreign debt which the Communist regime had managed to amass. The generous attitude to foreign investors and the *de facto* preference granted to them over local business people were part of the attempt of the first democratically elected government to avoid international insolvency and turn back the tide of indebtedness. This strategy seems to have borne fruit: throughout the transformation, Hungary has managed to maintain creditworthiness, and the level of foreign debt has been reduced from the terrifyingly high level of the second half of the 1980s. But the indebtedness has not gone away. The Hungarian state's debt to foreign fund holders has partly been transformed into indebtedness to *forint* holders. The fact is that *debt service currently represents 40 per cent of the total central government budget* (KSH 1997) - an enormous drain on public funds, which should instead go towards improving health, education and infrastructure, or be spent on regional development projects. The central budget's debt servicing obligations, alongside Hungary's unique negative demographic and public health situation, call for public revenues from Hungarian households and businesses. Foreign firms, and especially multinational businesses, do not pay much into the coffers of the Hungarian state: most of them received generous tax breaks from the outgoing Communist government under laws that were later (in 1993) very hard to phase out without upsetting the international community. The brunt of the tax burden rests with households, the consumer, and partly local businesses.

Other difficult aspects of transformation - such as the pressure on monetary policy in order to sterilise excessive growth in the money supply caused by strong capital inflows - do not need be discussed here at length, being similar in all relevant countries. Such sterilization is difficult and expensive; efforts by the central bank to neutralise the liquidity-creating effects of capital inflows result in a higher interest rate, and in its efforts to buy up securities from businesses and the general public, the bank runs expenditures on behalf of the central budget. The direct cost of sterilization will eventually be borne by the taxpayer, that is, by Hungarian households and businesses. As for the indirect costs, it is mainly local businesses that are affected by high real interest rates. Multinational firms and global banks functioning on the Hungarian market are not very sensitive to changes in monetary policy, as their funding base is world-wide, and can find ways to hedge Hungarian exchange-rate and interest-rate changes.

The position of FO-firms, however, differs according to the nature of their business. Surveys show that foreign investors represent three distinct types as far as their motives to invest in Hungary, as well as their perceptions of the obstacles are concerned. Group One consists of joint ventures whose main profile is to produce for the Hungarian market; they regard tax and social security expenditures as obstacle number 1, and inflation as obstacle number 2. Group Two includes foreign-owned firms that have assembly plants in Hungary for export purposes; their primary concern is general investment risk, and their secondary one is inflation. The third group identified in the survey consists of FO-firms which are export-oriented, based on a high local content: their main concern is inflation, followed by tax and social security contributions. The firms in the high export groups (2 and 3) do not regard exchange rate policy as a determining factor in their export activity (Elteto and Sass 1997). Their main dissatisfaction stems from the relatively high *inflation,* which stood in 1997[2]. Tight credit, poor banking services or the constant devaluation of the *forint,* however, affect foreign businessmen less than local entrepreneurs who cannot turn so easily to external banks for finance and services.

Conclusions

The first eight years of transformation in Hungary offer perhaps the fullest picture of foreign capital's *Janus-faced nature.* Rather by default than by any grand design, Hungary has opened up its economy more extensively than any other country in the region. As a result, the country has managed to secure an impressive amount of funds, particularly direct investments. These have certainly helped to accelerate the Schumpeterian "creative destruction" of old structures in industry, trade, finance and utilities. Massive inflows have helped successive Hungarian governments to reduce the level of external indebtedness. On the other hand, the short-term macro economic consequences of capital inflows aggravated key variables in the first few years, adding to unemployment and import intensity, and accelerated the shrinking of the market share of state-owned firms. As a consequence, public finances have suffered during the first half of the decade, both from loss of revenue and also from increased expenditure on unemployment benefit. These burdens came on top of those imposed by the inherited debt and the unavoidable costs of transition. Thus, throughout these years Hungary's macro economy remained somewhat unbalanced and sensitive to external judgement on her creditworthiness.

Concerning Hungary, it is intriguing that we have seen sizeable inflows into the productive sector, and the largest productivity gain in the region, but with no evidence of a commensurate rate of growth. The fact that the Hungarian economy has been the one with the slowest economic growth and the highest inflation rate among comparable CEE countries in the last three years despite the highest per capita stock of foreign direct capital should not make us jump to a wrong conclusion about the macro economic consequences of direct capital flows. The high overall cost of Hungarian labour partly explains the decline in employment. In 1995-96 there was a steep decline in real wages, following a government stabilization programme of questionable merit; such a further contraction of real wages and consumption was not planned, and certainly not justified in view of growing labour productivity during there years. My interpretation is that the unnecessary further drop in real wages as well as domestic consumption *and* investments were all unintended results of a higher-than-planned inflation rate in 1995-96 - a typical case of a policy overshoot. However, in spite of a drastic statistical improvement in international competitiveness thanks to lower unit labour costs, employment growth and investment have not accelerated. This remains a puzzle for those who underrate the importance of domestic markets in economic growth.

After some lags, the huge amount of capital absorbed will no doubt accelerate output and export growth; in fact, the first signs of dramatic growth have already appeared in certain industries during 1997. At present, however, growth seems to come from "islands" within Hungarian industry, and will not bring much improvement to important aspects of the economy and society such as employment or budgetary revenue. Regional imbalances will even grow wider, almost dividing the country into two parts. Future governments will face the difficult task of restoring certain regional and social balances, and reducing the *de facto* handicap of local businesses, particularly the SME sector, while the state is now devoid of practically all state assets which can be sold or used for structural/regional policy purposes. Modern production and financial clusters seem to have emerged around Budapest; these will have to keep up the momentum required to modernise various sectors of the economy. Yet in order to prosper a society needs more than that. Hungary needs a better health service, support for its still remarkably good educational system, and a closing of the gap between the rich and the poor. The country needs a dynamic local enterprise sector, which is willing and able to invest and recruit labour. It should also be made capable of saving more, and thus become less dependent on capital inflows - not because openness as such should be reduced, but because prosperity in the middle of Europe cannot be achieved in islands alone.

Notes

1   A trade-generating type of capital export has been so characteristic of Japanese foreign direct investments since the early 1970s that it is generally referred to as "Kojima-type" FDI after a publication on this phenomenon (Kojima 1973). The motive of such capital export is not to circumvent trade barriers, but to generate trade via relocation of the investor firms' production facilities into the (lower wage) target country.

2   In addition to the common factors of inflation during transition, here one should mention a particular feature of the Hungarian context. The 1995 privatization transactions mostly involved natural monopolies or near-monopolies (energy, telecommunications) and concessions in transport. Investors eager to secure a healthy yield on their multi-billion-dollar investments pressurised the government to increase utility rates and follow pre-agreed price increase formulae on toll roads. These efforts are reflected in consumer price index (CPI) increases: the overall CPI increase was 18.5 per cent in the first six months of 1997, but the rise for household energy was nearly 30 per cent, while only 8.7 per cent for consumer durables. A continued upward pressure in order to secure a high return on invested foreign funds will make it extremely hard for future Hungarian governments to bring inflation down to a single digit level.

References

Allami Privatizációs Vagyonkezelõ Rt. (1996), *Heti Privinfo*.
Blejer, M. & Coricelli, F. (1995), *The Making of Economic Reform in Eastern Europe*, Edward Elgar: Aldershot.

Bod, P. (1997), 'German Capital in Hungary: Is There a Special Relationship?', *Discussion Papers in German Studies*, Institute for German Studies: The University of Birmingham.

Diczházi, B., (1997), 'Külföldi tõkebefektetések hatása a regionális gazdaságra' [The Impact of FDI on the Regional Economy], *Privatizációs Kutatóintézet*, Budapest.

East-West Investment News (1995,1996), *Statistical Information*, Summer 1995, Autumn 1995, Summer 1996.

Eltetõ, A., Sass, M. (1997), 'A külföldi befektetõk döntéseit befolyásoló tényezõk' [Factors Influencing the Investment Decisions of Foreigners], *Közgazdasági Szemle*, Vol. XLIV., No.6, pp. 531-546.

European Bank for Reconstruction and Development (1995), *Transition Report*, London: EBRD.

---- (1996), *Transition Report*, London: EBRD.

---- (1997), *Transition Report*, London: EBRD.

Hungarian Central Statistical Office (1996), *Foreign Direct Investment in Hungary, 1994*, Budapest.

Hunya, G. (1996), 'Large Privatisation, Restructuring and Foreign Direct Investment', in Zecchini, S. (ed.), *Lessons from the Economic Transition - Central and Eastern Europe in the 1990s*, Kluwer Academic Publishers: London.

Kojima, K. (1973), *Direct Foreign Investment - A Japanese Model of Multinational Business Operation*, Pinter Publishers: London.

Krugman, P. (1991), *Geography and Trade*, MIT Press: Cambridge.

KSH (1997), *A KSH jelenti, 1997/6*, Central Statistical Office Publication, 22 August, pp.12-13.

PK=Privatizációs Kutatóintézet [Privatization Research Institute], *Helybenjárás és szabadesés* [Stagnation and Free Fall], Budapest, 1997.

Rostowski, J. (1996), 'Comparing Two Great Depressions: 1929-33 to 1989-93', in Zecchini, S. (ed.), *Lessons from the Economic Transition - Central and Eastern Europe in the 1990s*, Kluwer Academic Publishers: London.

Sass, M. (1997), *A közvetlen külföldi tõkebefektetések motivációinak változása és a magyar EU-tagság.* [Changes in Motivation of FDI and Hungarian Membership in the EU]. Világgazdasági Intézet, Budapest.

Simonian, H. (1997), 'Into the East at Full Throttle', *Financial Times*, 13 February.

Statistical Service of Ministry of Industry, Trade and Tourism, August 1997. Budapest,

World Bank (1996), *World Development Report*, Washington DC.

3 Investment promotion in the Czech Republic, Hungary and Poland

Anne-Ev Enzmann

Introduction

Today, at the end of the 20th century, nation states in Europe are competing more for the means to create wealth within their boundaries than for power over additional territory. Not only firms are fighting for markets, but governments equally compete for investors. At the beginning of the transition process away from the planned economy towards market-oriented systems, policy-makers and Western consultants were enthusiastic about the role FDI could play in Central and Eastern Europe. After FDI had been restricted in almost all former Comecon-countries, reform governments recognized FDI as an important development strategy to upgrade their national economies in order to gain competitiveness and integrate into world markets. Meanwhile it is evident that expectations have not (yet) been met. Many foreign investors are still reluctant to enter the new markets by FDI. The urgently needed FDI to restructure the economy and sustain economic reforms has failed to materialize on a large scale. Hungary, the Czech Republic and Poland are the region's spearheads. Yet in comparison to the annual FDI inflows into the rapidly growing South Eastern Asian economies, they are significantly lagging behind (Dobosiewicz, 1992).

It is thus time to assess the role FDI can play in Central and Eastern European transition countries. The aim of this contribution is to shed light on two crucial questions for policy-makers: (i) What are possibilities and limitations for facilitating and regulating FDI today? (ii) Can multinational corporations (MNCs) be harnessed for development policies? The intention is to make a contribution to the broader discussion on the role of the nation state in competing for investment in the global arena. The analysis thus tries to contribute to the debate of political control and autonomy of the state *vis-à-vis* MNCs. Can, and if so how, and to what extent - host governments promote investment and influence investment decisions of MNCs?

The hypothesis of this article is that intensifying, global competition for FDI has made governments around the globe lose bargaining power to multinationals. Yet, there is scope for strategic investment promotion beyond inflation control and low tax rates under carefully defined objectives (Artisien *et al.* 1993). The distribution of costs and benefits between MNCs and governments depends mainly on the bargaining power of the latter. The approach of this paper is an empirical micro-analysis of the experience with FDI in the Czech Republic, Poland and Hungary. Based on field interviews and alongside the pursuit of a sample of published case studies between 1994 and 1996, the study takes a behavioral perspective on foreign investors and governments in order to analyze foreign investors' strategies, host government's policies and the relationship of the two (Alter and Wehrle 1993). The paper will start with the foreign investors' point of view: (i) What strategies do MNCs pursue entering Central and Eastern Europe? (ii) What attracts them specifically to Poland, Hungary or the Czech Republic? (iii) Why do other MNCs hesitate? A second part will then assess the impact of FDI. Against this background, a third part will analyze policy options and dilemmas for investment promotion. Last, the contribution seeks to answer the question about the relationship between individual governments and MNCs.

Multinational corporations in Central and Eastern Europe

Scholars offer a whole cocktail of paradigms, yet no theory of determinants and motives exists which could fully explain, within a single equation, all kinds of FDI activities (Dunning 1992). Empirical research and case-studies on the region of Central and Eastern Europe point out three major FDI strategies:

- Access to local and/or regional markets;

- Low-cost production for exports and strategic sourcing;

- Global strategy: global market share.

When foreign investors in Poland and the Czech Republic were asked why they entered the region, most of them described their primary goal as gaining access to local and regional markets. Examples for this most frequent type of FDI are *Unilever, Colgate-Palmolive, Philips, Alcatel, PepsiCo, GM, Fiat, Nestle, Ikea, Volkswagen, Deutsche Telekom, Siemens*[1]. The second most important motive for market entry by FDI was to exploit Central and Eastern Europe's low wage, but well-qualified labour force for competitive export production. To illustrate: *Thomson*, the world-wide number two television tube producer, is selling more than 50 percent of the tubes made at the Warsaw plant through its European sales network. *Philips* exports more than 50 percent of the lighting equipment towards the EU after having transferred a certain type of battery production from Belgium to Poland. *Matsushita Electric Industrial Co.* (brand names are *Panasonic* and *Technics*) is planning to serve the entire European market from its new site in the Czech Republic (Czech Invest 1995).

Often the motive of using the region as a low cost basis for exports is intertwined with increasing market share in the region itself. *Asea Brown Boveri* (ABB), the Swedish-Swiss technical engineering company, is a prime example for this double approach. The expansion into Central and Eastern Europe by FDI provides:

1. Access to a huge potential market, which lacks almost every product ABB, makes (railways, power plants, airports, industrial plants etc.).

2. The production facilities in the region are important low cost suppliers in the company's global outsourcing strategy.

3. Drawing on the extensive experience of BBC in the region before 1989, ABB has created 70 affiliates employing altogether 23.000 employees in the region since 1990. ABB plants in the Czech Republic and Poland have taken over substantial production from subsidiaries in Germany and Switzerland. Half of the machine tools ABB uses in power plants for the South-East-Asian market are supplied by ABB subsidiaries from Central and Eastern Europe. ABB intends to make its Polish joint venture factories the sole producer of special turbines for energy-saving power plants. Sales in the region were up to $2bn for 1996.

Similarly, the investment of Italian car-giant *Fiat* has been driven both by low costs and the existence of a large domestic market, in which uncertainty is reduced by decades of previous experience. Fiat integrated its Polish subsidiary into its global network of production and now manufactures the model *Uno* exclusively in Poland with three-quarters of the production being sold to the parent company.

Following Dunning (1992), a third type of FDI can be identified as 'strategic asset seeking'. This strategy goes beyond the simple motive of gaining access to domestic markets, but takes a global view on market presence (Artisien *et al.* 1993). In this respect, FDI in Central and Eastern Europe is a means to consolidate market presence and enhance competition for customers and markets on a global scale. Immediate profitability or quick return on investments may be less important than long-term goals such as globally recognized brand names, and global market leadership. *Fiat*, for example, did not only look for the local Polish market and a low cost base for exports, but also pursues long-term strategic objectives: (i) competition against rivals, and (ii) a larger share of European and worldwide car production. Accordingly, foreign investment in the privatization process is dominated by acquisitions of domestic firms with market power. The acquisition of FSM in Poland, for example, guaranteed Fiat a market share of 53 percent (Hany 1995).

According to Hunya (1992), three main features determine foreign investors' decisions about an investment location in Central and Eastern Europe:

- *Market potential*: market size and growth potential;

- *Risk assessment*: political and economic stability - reliability   of the reform process;

- *Availability of skilled* (and still relatively cheap) *labour*.

Hungary is still the region's spearhead as regards total inflows of FDI (see also the previous contribution by P. Bod in this volume). Its success can generally be explained in terms of its stable business environment. Since FDI was already allowed under the so-called *Gulyas communism*, foreign companies found it relatively easy to embark on new FDI projects. Offering clear market-oriented reforms and a strong commitment towards privatization and foreign investment, foreign companies such as *Siemens* and *GM* started expanding into Central and Eastern European via Hungary. *Siemens* then continued into the Czech Republic, while Poland followed as the third investment location.

The Czech Republic primarily attracted FDI due to its impressive track record of political and economic stability during 1990-1997. Until the elections in June 1996, Vaclav Klaus' Czech Republic was *le bon élève de la classe*, (i) offering a single-digit inflation rate, (ii) being the first country to join the OECD, (iii) having a balanced budget, and (iv) obtaining from the international credit rating agency *Moody's* an A certification. *Matsushita*, a Japanese investor known for being cautious, opted in early 1996 for the Czech Republic as its first location in the region - although it did not get the expected incentives it lobbied for. Matsushita was to establish a green field plant in Pilsen manufacturing TVs for export to the European market, employing about 350 people (Czech Invest 1995). Poland's locational advantages are its market size and prospects for growth as well as its central location in Europe including the proximity to the Russian market. As a representative of GM confirmed: "Poland has two main locational advantages, the largest economy and the best growth rates" in the region (quotation taken from personal interview).

When foreign enterprises were asked about major impediments, they indicated two major constraints:

- The unstable and insufficiently developed legal and regulatory system;

- The lack of transparent public decision making.

Especially Poland's political turmoil between 1991 and 1994 adversely affected foreign investors. The long-stalled privatization as well as the hassles of doing business locally contributed to make Poland the *Visegrad's* laggard in attracting FDI. Foreign investors are discouraged by having to deal with a revolving door of bureaucrats, changes at lower levels of the ministerial hierarchy as well as regulatory constraints, often changing legislation and legal lacunas open to interpretation (Hyclak and King 1994, p. 535). Thus, uncertainty and risk can make foreign investors postpone their projects ('wait and see option'), withdraw from negotiations or try to reduce risk by minimizing their upfront capital investment. A MNC active in the chemical industry in Poland did not bring its latest technology, but made its contribution rather in kind: an old plant from former East Germany was transferred to Poland in 1991. An official explained:

> I want political stability - stability not only at the very top, but also within the bureaucracy. It is difficult to plan and develop business strategies, if the responsible government official, with whom I spoke yesterday, is already replaced tomorrow - and this continuously (quotation taken from personal interview).

The resulting problem for transition countries is that the obstacle 'uncertainty' especially affects capital and technology-intensive production, which requires a long-term commitment. These are the engagements Central and Eastern Europe is starving for. Less affected are labour-intensive, low technology production, such as textiles or services, where the investor can easily withdraw. Uncertainty is accepted if opportunity costs of postponement are higher than the option of wait and see.

The Role of FDI - Performance and Impact

Despite investors' interest in Central and Eastern Europe, FDI flows to the region is still rather disappointing. In 1994 Central and Eastern Europe as well as the Newly Independent States, with a population of 400 million people, attracted as much FDI as Malaysia alone with its 19 million inhabitants (EBRD 1995, p. 6). FDI primarily concentrated on Hungary, the Czech Republic, Poland and Russia.

Table 9
FDI in Central and Eastern Europe (in millions US $)

	1992	1993	1994	1995	1989-1995	per capita 1989-95	per capita 1995	% of GDP
Hungary	1,471	2,339	1,146	4,100	11,013	1,069	398	6,3
Czech Republic	983	517	850	2,500	5,481	532	243	3,1
Poland	284	580	542	900	2,423	63	23	0,4
Russia	700	400	1,000	1,500	3,100	21	10	0,2

Source: EBRD (1996, p. 116).

Hungary is still the region's spearhead attracting up to $11bn as of the end of 1995. The total amount of FDI in the Czech Republic amounted to $5.4bn at the end of 1995. The huge upsurge in FDI in 1995 was helped by the acquisition of 27 percent of *SPT Telecom* by *Swiss Telecom* and *PTT Telecom* (The Netherlands), who paid as a consortium $1.45bn. Poland is still lagging behind Hungary and the Czech Republic despite a domestic market, which is four times as big as the aforesaid. FDI reached $2.4bn at the end of 1995. FDI per capita was only 23$.

Transfer of know-how

Interviews in privatized Polish enterprises subject to FDI revealed a tremendous transfer of know-how and skills in almost all areas of

51

operation. Transfers occur in form of technology, manufacturing and marketing know-how as well as in the form of organizational and managerial skills. MNCs are key channels for the cross-border transfer of culture and business customs and have invested in training and career development with determination. The most radical changes have taken place within management and in the area of quality control. Restructuring programs by foreign investors do not merely introduce new organizational structures, western management techniques and technology, but equally build up a new corporate culture based on competitiveness, responding to consumers' needs, markets' prerogatives as well as quality control and cost reduction.

Given the competitive advantage of low labour costs, foreign investors in Central and Eastern Europe typically engage in labour-intensive, low-tech production. Since manufacturing sectors, such as automobiles, electronics or computers, are required to integrate internationally in order to compete successfully for efficient manufacturing, MNCs do not undertake substantial R&D, but continue centralizing innovation in a Western location. Having introduced new products, quality control and increased productivity, MNCs can make exports more competitive. So far, the majority of Polish MNCs is focused at the local markets. Hungary's MNCs, however, successfully boasted the country's exports. While foreign investment represents 10 percent of GDP, it accounted for 50 percent of export sales in 1993, and is now estimated at 70 percent (Business Central Europe 1996, p. 42).

Spillover effects on local entrepreneurs, suppliers and competitors concerning organizational and work practices are even more important than direct effects of FDI on companies concerned. Initially, islands of modern management and firms achieving outstanding productivity and product quality arise, thus prompting strategic investors to seek the restructuring of ever-larger parts of an industry. Since the Czech, Hungarian and Polish cost structure are proving advantageous to local suppliers, almost all companies surveyed tried as much as possible to source locally. In the interest of foreign companies, component suppliers are trained and helped to meet Western quality standards. Evidently, FDI puts competitive pressure on such local firms.

To illustrate the point in more detail: the example of *Volkswagen* (VW) in the Czech Republic shows that the German investor not only restructured *Škoda Automoliová* from the bottom-up. Within a short period of time the whole supplier chain was equally reorganized. Sourcing in the Czech Republic led to tremendous increases in quality standards and productivity. Until today, more than 60 foreign suppliers of VW have followed the carmaker into the Czech Republic. They set up business either in the form of joint ventures with locals or opted for green field investments. In the meantime, the Czech suppliers are fully integrated into the global sourcing network of VW. Equally, Škoda has access to all VW- suppliers. Furthermore, it is foreseeable that Czech suppliers, trained by VW and having qualified for delivering in-time, will also supply other car makers, such as *General Motors* or *Daewoo*, both of which produce across the border in Poland. FDI in the automotive sector amounts to one quarter of all FDI in the Czech Republic. Approximately 10 to 15 percent are held by the supplier industry. However, there are limits to local content. MNCs cannot afford to compromise quality standards in their supply chain. In the case of the *VW-Škoda* alliance, the former sources low-tech components locally, with foreign suppliers dominating in areas of design, development and sophisticated electronic components (e.g. air conditioning, ABS, power steering).

Industry structure and competitiveness

The expansion of MNCs into the region has transformed domestic markets, often augmenting the dominant positions of MNCs. In the Polish food processing sector, for example, classic oligopolistic characteristics of collusion and rivalry are exhibited (Hardy 1994, p. 31). The case of the tea sector illustrates how the entry of *Unilever* and *Tetley* reduced competition to a two-horse race. After the state-owned monopoly lost its right for exclusive distribution in 1989, a large number of independent suppliers set up direct contacts to Indian tea producers. However, this neo-classical notion of a market with many suppliers, none of whom could influence the price, was quickly brought to an end. Supported by heavy advertising, which was relatively cheap compared to Western standards, but expensive for a Polish company with little capital, two MNCs segmented the market: *Unilever's* Lipton tea as an up market brand, and *Tetley's* aimed at the mass market (ibid.).

Additionally, if special market protection is granted as in the case of *Fiat* in Poland, FDI may in the short run promote protectionism instead of competition. Fiat and GM demanded higher tariffs on automobile imports as a condition for their joint venture.

Given the strategy of multinational enterprises to acquire local market leaders and well-known brands, there is always a tendency to dominate the respective market. Especially in privatization capital entering prefers protected industries. In Hungary, more than a third of FDI has gone into branches where full competition hardly exists (Vissi 1994). Thus, FDI strategies by multinationals, which seek to protect their market influence and thereby grow to monopolists or oligopolists amongst a few big companies, drive smaller local companies out of business. In addition, a huge gap has opened up between MNCs and local enterprises in Hungary, the largest FDI recipient. There seem to be few spill over effects, but a dramatic dichotomy between competitive MNCs and ailing local companies (Business Central Europe 1996, p. 42). On the other hand, FDI can encourage the development of indigenous players. Polish enterprises operating in the chemical sector are performing rather well under foreign-induced competitive pressure. *Pollena Lechia* for example, a Polish household detergent producer, successfully competes with *Henkel* and *Unilever* (Business Central Europe 1995, p. 34).

Preliminary conclusions

FDI has overtaken trade as the driving force in Central and East European countries' integration into the world markets. The impact of FDI on economic development in Hungary, Poland and the Czech Republic can be described as a 'mixed bag'. FDI is not in itself beneficial for the development of the host country's economy. As empirical evidence shows, FDI by MNCs is not *per se* a means towards de-monopolization and increased competitiveness. Multinationals can assume substantial market influence, and tend to oligopolistic behavior that may be detrimental to emerging markets (Gareffi and Newfarmer 1995). However case studies have also shown how FDI can be extremely valuable. Foreign investment can be a powerful means to support the transition process. Direct and indirect effects energize industrial restructuring, and provide channels for technological change, introduction of management know-how and extended market penetration.

As a matter of fact, efficiency has increased sharply in the companies, which were surveyed. Yet, to be able to assess the specific contribution of FDI, one has to compare these achievements to the performance of firms with domestic investors. Case studies help draw a clearer conclusion. Comparing two Polish companies, where the foreign investors *Thomson* and *Gerber* have taken a majority share, with three privatized enterprises owned by Polish investors (the *Krosno Glassworks*, *Tonsil* and the *Slaka* cable and wire factory), the relative lack of success of the latter three can be attributed to deficiencies in marketing, finance and cost accounting - in other words, areas in which there is a lack of Western expertise (Mc Donald 1993). Furthermore, empirical evidence from the *Gdansk Institute for Market Economics* shows that there is a significant investment gap between foreign and domestically privatized enterprises (Center for Social and Economic Research 1995). In general, foreign buyers invest ten times as much as domestic buyers (personal interview with the former Polish Minister for Privatization, Mr. Lewandowski).

Host governments' FDI policies: options and dilemmas

One of the pivotal questions asked by policy makers in Central and Eastern Europe concerns the following: What are the possibilities and limitations for promoting and regulating FDI? More specifically, how can transition economies in post-communist countries successfully compete in the global arena for FDI, and harness such resources for their respective development. In short, what is the experience with FDI in the Czech Republic, Poland and Hungary to date? The pros and cons of different policy options shall be discussed in the following section against the background of experiences made in the three aforementioned countries.

Interviews with foreign investors in Poland and the Czech Republic confirm findings in other studies that incentives are often ineffective, but difficult to avoid as appetizers (OECD 1995). On the one hand, incentives such as tax holidays, tax reductions, subsidized credit or capital grants, tariff protection or reduction etc. involves a variety of direct and indirect costs. Most importantly, they erode the governments' revenue base without any corresponding benefit to the host country. On the other hand, incentives packages cannot overcome and compensate for the fundamental obstacles to FDI such as political instability or a lack of clear policy regulation. To illustrate, tax relief for companies reduce revenues while there is strong evidence to suggest that many investors would have invested anyway. The Czech experience provides support for the hypothesis that resources are better targeted to develop the legal and institutional infrastructure, and offering a clear tax system than providing incentives, which are geared towards influencing investment decisions. Managers consistently rank political and economic risks higher than government incentives.

However, one should not ignore the fact that there are a number of cases where incentives do play a decisive role for an investment decision. Highly mobile green field investments like automotive or electronics tariffs and quotas have proven an effective incentive to make foreign investors manufacture in small domestic markets. Still, a follow-up problem may subsequently arise: the pressure for more incentives to the investor as soon as the reason for granting the initial incentives is gone.

A recent example from *Daewoo*, the South Korean industrial group, who is the single largest private investor in Central and Eastern Europe, highlights the kind of behavior this may bread. After acquiring a 40 percent stake in *Kazakhtelecom*, Kazakhstan's telecommunications monopoly in 1997 as part of the country's privatization program, *Daewoo* sold the entire stake in March 1998 to *Kazkommerts Securities*, an investment bank based in the country's capital city, Almaty. In the wake of South Korea's prevailing macro-economic difficulties, *Daewoo's* action may appear reasonable. The industrial group had promised to pay $1.37bn, which included a $1bn investment to increase the number of phone lines in Kazakhstan from 2m to 3.3m by 2.000. But the ambitious investment plans had to be delayed, and subsequently called into question the industrial group's expanding strategies in Poland and the Ukraine. In February 1998, for instance, *Daewoo* signed a joint venture agreement with the Ukrainian factory *Avtozaz*, in which the former promised to invest $1.3bn over several years - a figure that would nearly double the total foreign direct investment in Ukraine since independence in 1991. As a condition for the deal, however, the Ukrainian government had to implement restrictions on the import of used cars and grant *Daewoo* extensive tax holidays. This incentives package has angered the *European Commission*, and could hurt Ukraine's chances for membership in the *World Trade Organization* (Financial Times 1998a).

In order to achieve specific development objectives governments in Hungary, Poland and the Czech Republic have linked the granting of incentives to carefully targeted performance requirements. However, it must be born in mind that such requirements involve direct and indirect costs.

- Requiring local content;

- Promoting exports;

- Promoting R&D;

- Attracting investment to low-growth regions;

- Creating or maintaining employment.

Regarding the *local content requirement*, the following example illustrates the argument. In 1997 the Polish government made market entry of three international telecommunication operators - *AT&T*, *Alcatel* and *Siemens* - dependent on the condition that domestic companies supplied 50 percent of the value of communications equipment. While the government successfully imposed a local content requirement, the foreign investor might thus have to bear a (temporary) loss in production efficiency, and could therefore be deterred. MNCs in the automotive sector for example opt less and less for national suppliers, but pursue global sourcing strategies, thereby leaving little room for governments' intervention in favour of domestic firms (Frydman *et al.* 1993).

To illustrate, *Continental*, the German tire manufacturer, was one of the first companies to move into Eastern Europe. Its site in the Czech Republic produces more *Conti* care tires than any of its other plants. Its decision to move into Russia, announced in mid-March 1998, is the next step in its globalization drive. These moves are in part a reflection of *Conti's* need to follow its customers - the big car makers - as they push into new, fast-growing markets. To date, *Conti's* business is confined mostly to the relatively mature economies of Western Europe, with only a small exposure to fast-growing emerging markets. The globalization drive is being made possible by a new process being developed by *Continental* called a *modular manufacturing process* (MMP). Basic tire parts (modules) are manufactured in low-cost locations such as Hungary and the Czech Republic, then shipped to markets where they are sold for assembly according to customers' requirements. The established factories in Hungary and the Czech Republic as well as the new one in Russia use MMP (Financial Times 1998b).

As a general rule, local content requirements are a useful means to provide for more spillover effects on the host country's supplier industry. This policy forces companies to upgrade their suppliers, provide assistance and train their personnel in order to meet quality standards and delivery times. However, the sourcing strategies of many foreign companies are already in favour of Central European suppliers since the latter have the competitive advantage of cheaper labour costs. *General Motors'* purchasing team, for instance, plans to localize up to 70 percent of its parts and components production (Central European Automotive Report 1996). Yet, as the cases of *ABB* and *VW-Skoda* show, it takes time to bring Central and East European suppliers up to Western standards. Thus, the propensity of foreign companies to buy from local firms is very much dependent on the latter's capability to adjust - sooner rather than later - to Western performance requirements.

There is further evidence to suggest that incentives to *promote export*-oriented investment tend to be a relatively effective form of securing investment. Export oriented production, as for example in electronics or other labour-intensive sectors, is attracted by low-cost environments. While the most important local cost factor in these industries is labour, tax regulations may equally form a significant parameter (OECD 1995). As experience in Hungary has shown, this kind of export-oriented, labour-intensive investment is especially sensitive to taxation, and thus susceptible for tax incentives. The Hungarian approach can be regarded as successful on the basis of export oriented investors being attracted to the emerging market. The costs in the short-term are small, since several of these investors would not have come without the tax exemptions.

However, at the same time Hungarian export promotion policies illustrate a variety of constraints, especially in the long run. Having established special economic zones where green field investments are dispensed from customs duties and other taxes to import machinery, components and raw materials for assembly and re-export, Hungary succeeded in attracting significant volumes in FDI. Yet, the price tag attached to this achievement is significant. Since foreign investment remains off shore when concentrated in such duty-free zones, this policy limits both the creation of linkages to local companies and the establishment of spillover effects on the domestic industry. The fact that Hungarian companies fare worse than Czech or Polish ones under foreign imposed competition points to the risks involved in this export promotion policy (Business Central Europe 1996). Moreover, these investments tend to be footloose, meaning that they move on as soon as the incentive has expired, *ipso facto* served its purpose.

Regional policy making with the help of FDI is, as the Polish example may illustrate, ambiguous. Attempts to attract investors through incentive schemes to underdeveloped regions, i.e. to the eastern provinces of Poland, in order to diminish regional discrepancies, have not proven very successful. Despite heavy campaigning and the offering of tax incentives, FDI in Poland remains clustered in highly urbanized *voivodships* (administrative shorthand for regions). The largest number of firms with foreign capital are registered in the Warsaw, followed by Poznan, Gdansk, Katowice, Szczecin and Wroclaw *voivodships*. *Voivodships* located in Eastern Poland on the borders to Belarus and Ukraine are lagging significantly behind. Insufficient infrastructure, unattractive location to western markets and a lack of other industries make MNCs reluctant from choosing these regions as an investment location. Conversely, picking urbanized regions offering a solid infrastructure, an efficient administration and proximity to other industries may provide the ‚package deal' that tilts the balance. Governments can influence these choices. If they want to bring FDI to these regions, national and/or local government agencies have to invest *beforehand* in infrastructure projects. Such public policy making plays a vital role in supporting and stimulating private investment, no matter if foreign or domestic in origin (EBRD 1996, p. 33ff.).

Maintaining and creating employment through FDI is a major concern of governments in transition countries. Some examples underline the importance. Almost all of *Audi's* engines – a subsidiary of *VW* – come from a spotless new plant in Györ, western Hungary. Workers there earn about one-sixth of the rates in German manufacturing. In 1998 *Audi* also plans to start assembling cars in Hungary, underlining the quality, as well as the low cost, of workers there (Inzelt 1994, p. 141ff). *VW*, meanwhile, has shifted production to Slovakia, where wages are up to a quarter lower than at Wolfsburg, its headquarters in Lower Saxony, Germany. A commitment to safeguarding and/or creating a target number of jobs constituted part of the agreement to locate FDI. Furthermore, in the case of *San*, a high-profile Polish biscuit maker company, *McVities* (UK) agreed in 1996 to retain part of the management personnel, and gave workers a four-year job guarantee.

While the Polish government was able to oblige such conditions on *McVities*, investors are often unwilling or hesitant to make these concessions in the case of less attractive companies. Since a loss in efficiency of production and managerial decision making capacity is at stake, it will frequently involve considerable 'sweeteners' from the respective governments in order to attract such investments. While granting tax incentives in exchange for employment conditions, the host government runs the risk of being exposed to repeated pressure for additional incentives by the beneficiary firm as soon as the reason for granting the first incentive is gone. Finally, sanction mechanisms against firms not honoring their commitments are rather ambiguous since their threat or effective application may deter other prospective investors (Healey 1994).

Experience in the Czech Republic equally shows that marketing a transition country can make a difference. The success of *Czech Invest*, the Czech agency for foreign investment promotion, is due to a clearly defined goal: attracting green field investment in strategic sectors of the Czech economy. *Czech Invest* has focused on the automotive, electrical engineering, electronics and chemical industries. The Czech experience also underlines that investment promotion is most effective for companies that manufacture exports, since these are the firms facing real choices of where to go (OECD 1993, p. 46). However, it should be borne in mind that *Czech Invest* would not have been that successful if the country's policies during 1992 and 1996 had not been conducive to FDI.

Conclusions

A first conclusion can thus be drawn. All three Central European governments are eager to attract FDI. However, while they pursue common goals, the Czech, Hungarian and Polish governments have chosen different policies to reach the objective - not least due to different preconditions at the start of the transition process. Hungary is heavily indebted and struggled with double-digit unemployment until 1997. The Gyula Horn government, in office between 1994 and 1998, introduced a wide-ranging incentives policy in order to maintain its high levels of FDI. By contrast, the government of Vaclav Klaus in the Czech Republic, in office until autumn of 1997, repeatedly prided itself of an unemployment rate reaching only 3 percent. In addition, the Klaus administration inherited no foreign debt burden as in Hungary. Conversely, it has also courted foreign investors, but exercised caution in the provision of generous incentives packages (OECD 1993, p. 71). Poland could be seen to stand somewhere in the middle of both countries. Political turmoil and unclear policy provisions have frequently characterized the dynamics of foreign investment. Whilst it is too early to assess which Central European country will fare better in a long term perspective, the prevailing investment climate helps in explaining the early successes of Hungary and the Czech Republic.

On a more general level it is imperative that clear policy goals are formulated when attracting foreign investors. For instance, investment promotion policies in the emerging markets of Central and Eastern Europe face constraints that cannot easily be ignored. They can easily run into dilemmas of choice. Thus, host countries should use the instrument of administrative discretion. Based on an individual, carefully conducted cost - benefits analysis, investment promotion policies can be tailored to the individual project, thereby avoiding unnecessary incentives. The definition of clear policy goals entails to identify strategic industries, which are attractive to foreign investors and benefit the national economy. Promoting export-oriented investment has proven to be the most effective and least harmful. The choice of the right partner is critical in this context. FDI is not *per se* beneficial. Its success also depends upon the characteristics of the foreign investors. In short, foreign monopolists are as bad as local ones (Mc Millan 1995).

Last but not least. Policy makers in transition economies need to be (made) aware of the limitations of FDI. FDI cannot replace an overall development strategy as regards privatization proceedings, legal and administrative coherence, political stability, and continuity of personnel policies. Since FDI will tend to be selective, those sectors that are less affected from capital inflows will require target specific public policies (Healey 1994). It has frequently been observed, and criticized, that foreign investors only engage in privatization projects of companies and sectors, which are potentially highly profitable, thus leaving the unprofitable parts and industrial segments in the hand of the state. This "cherry-picking exercise" is a policy dilemma difficult to avoid for governments in emerging markets. In other words, sectoral and regional priorities of foreign investors may not follow the government's emphasis (Köves 1992, p. 54).

Note

1   Interviews with representatives from these firms were conducted in Poland, the Czech Republic and Hungary between Spring 1995 and Spring 1996. I am greatly indebted to the editor, Dr Jens Bastian, for making substantial suggestions and revisions to the contribution.

References

Artisien, P., Rojec M. and Svetlicic, M. (1993/eds), *Foreign Investment in Central and Eastern Europe*, St. Martin's Press: New York.

Alter, R. and Wehrle, F. (1993), Foreign Direct Investment in Central and Eastern Europe. An Assessment of the Current Situation, in *Intereconomics*, May/June, pp. 126-186.

Business Central Europe (1995), *Poland Survey*, February issue.

---- (1996), *Foreign Investment Survey*, April issue, pp. 39-52.

Center for Social and Economic Research (1995), *Foreign Privatization in Poland*, Studies & Analysis 30, Warsaw.

Central European Automotive Report (1996), Vol. 1, Issue 2.

Czech Invest (1995), *Annual Report 1995*, Czech Invest: Prague.

Dobosiewicz, Z. (1992), *Foreign Investment in Eastern Europe*, Routledge: London.

Dunning, J. H. (1992), *Multinational Enterprises and the Global Economy*, Addison-Wesley Publishers Ltd.: Wokingham.

EBRD (1995), *Transition Report*, EBRD: London.

---- (1996), *Transition Report*, EBRD: London.

Financial Times (1998a), Daewoo Sells Part of 40 % Kazakh Stake.

---- (1998b), Continental Chairman Follows Cost-Cutting Route to Recovery.

Frydman, R., Rapaczynski, A. and Earle, J. S. (1993/eds.), *The Privatization Process in Central Europe*, Central European University Press: London.

Gareffi, G. and Newfarmer, R.S. (1995), International Oligopoly and Uneven Development: Some Lessons From Industrial Case Studies, in Gomes-Casseres, B. and Yoffie D.B. (eds.), *The International Political Economy of FDI*, Vol. I, The Library of International Political Economy 4, p. 250-272.

Hardy, J. (1994), Eastern Promise? Foreign Investment in Poland, in *European Business Review*, Vol. 94, No.5, pp. 28-37.

Hany, C. (1995), Foreign Direct Investment in Central Eastern Europe. Some Lessons for Poland from Hungary, in *Intereconomics*, Vol. 30, pp. 36-43.

Healey, N. M. (1994), Doing Business with Eastern Europe. A Situational Analysis, in *European Business Review*, Vol. 94, No. 3, pp. 3-8.

Hunya, G. (1992), Foreign Direct Investment and Privatization in Central and Eastern Europe, in *Communist Economies and Economic Transformation*, Vol. 4, No. 4, pp. 501-511.

Hyclak, T. J. and King, A. E. (1994), The Privatization Experience in Eastern Europe, in *World Economy*, Vol. 17, No. 4, pp. 317-342.

Inzelt, A. (1994), Privatization and Innovation in Hungary: First Experiences, in *Economic Systems*, Vol. 18, Issue 2, pp. 141-158.

Mc Donald, K.R. (1993), Why Privatization is not Enough, in *Harvard Business Review*, May-June issue.

Mc Millan, C. H. (1995), Foreign Direct Investment in Eastern Europe: Harnessing FDI to the Transition from Plan to Market, in Chan, S. (ed.), *Foreign Direct Investment in a Changing Global Political Economy*, St Martin's Press: New York, pp. 127-149.

Köves, A. (1992), *Central and East European Economies in Transition. The International Dimension*, Westview Press: London.

OECD (1993), *Promoting FDI in Developing Countries*, OECD: Paris.

---- (1995), *Taxation and Foreign Direct Investment*. OECD: Paris.

Vissi, F. (1994), Foreign Direct Investment and Competition, *Institute for World Economics, Hungarian Academy of Science*, Working Papers No. 31.

4 Introducing private pension funds in transition economies of Central Europe

Jens Bastian

Introduction

Private pension funds and social insurance reform are attracting critical attention in OECD countries. As a central element in the process to reform welfare states, identify governments' role as provider of basic pensions, and argue the economic case for moving from a pay-as-you-go system (PAYG) to funded, individually-owned pensions, the scope and character of the debate is timely. In a word, social-security privatization is high on policy agendas. But the geography of the debate on pension reform does not stop in Western Europe! As part of the wider challenge to rebuild social insurance systems, pension reform is one of the *key reform issues* which governments in East and Central Europe must confront sooner than later. The urgency of the task is further informed by the need to build up a diverse pool of private pension funds so that there will be a larger demand for long-term assets to match longer-term pension liabilities.

The political economy of pension funding - and reform - in Central and Eastern Europe faces numerous problems, which are addressed in more detail in the course of this contribution. Their state pension schemes are financed out of current tax revenues, implicitly establishing a generational contract between today's contributors and tomorrow's pensioners. Hence, the *insurance function* of pensions is concentrated in the hands of state institutions. In short, principles of insurance are mixed with solidarity between generations. However, the strain on these schemes is exasperated by a plurality of factors. Under conditions of unprecedented economic and social change, these systems are struggling for viability as a proportionally smaller number of active workers must support an ever-growing number of [early] pensioners. The latter's life expectancy is forecast to slowly increase again the more the transition process is consolidated and delivers the promised economic goods. At present, many people in transition economies of Central and Eastern Europe are too poor and/or too short-sighted to save enough for their old-age retirement, while others are still confident that their respective governments will look after them when they can draw their state pension. Still, without huge tax increases such PAYG systems are unsustainable.

The major hypothesis to be elaborated in this contribution consists in the argument that the crises can act as a catalyst for change. Declining standards of living in old age during the transition process leaves little margin for trimming existing benefits. Faced with the equally untenable prospect of tax increases in order to further prolong the agony of PAYG systems before their eventual meltdown, some Central and Eastern European countries are moving towards establishing a multi-pillar pensions system in which PAYG elements are concentrated on providing subsistence benefits (*poverty relief objective*). Empirical examples from Poland and Hungary that highlight the pool of changes gradually gaining currency, endeavor to underwrite this hypothesis. With the introduction of private pension funds the aforementioned insurance function of pensions (provided by the state), can be separated from the *savings function*, for which the private sector is responsible. Furthermore, through the operation of private pension funds borrowers (institutional and/or individuals) can seek an alternative source of finance, making the financial systems of transition economies as a whole less dependent on the discretionary decisions of a still volatile banking sector.

Catalysts for change

Establishing supplementary pension-savings schemes will be a milestone in the transition economies of Central and Eastern European countries. The switch from a singular system to a multi-pillar system will not automatically solve the existing pension crisis. Domestic and external forces drive the need for the reform process. Among the latter are multi-national institutions such as the *International Monetary Fund* (IMF), the *World Bank*, and the *EU Commission*. Additionally, foreign financial institutions are targeting a region of emerging markets whose demand for insurance looks certain to grow as a result of ongoing macro-economic stabilization and regulatory liberalization. In what follows, the contribution shall seek to address a variety of inter-connected issues about social insurance reforms in transition economies. These issues concern:

- The status of pension reforms in Central and Eastern Europe. In Central and Eastern Europe, older people have been affected by the fall in output and have experienced a decline in their average living standards. In Hungary, for instance, pensioners have been hardest hit by tough austerity measures launched in 1995, with the real value of pensions falling by a quarter between 1995 and 1996 (Eddy 1998). There is a case on equity grounds for being generous to today's elderly, and in many countries they have been relatively well protected, for instance in Poland. But the multitude of pensioners can create a vicious circle in which high pension spending leads to high payroll contributions, incentives not to declare employment, and thus stagnating or falling government revenue.

- The increasing role of private provisions. Funded schemes combine past contributions with interests, dividends and capital gains, amounting to a lump sum when the individual retires. This quantity is then converted into an annuity. Funded schemes therefore combine *saving* (during the working life) with *insurance* (the annuity).

- Mandatory versus voluntary participation in private pension funds. Given the degree of uncertainty and risk in post-communist societies, the willingness to make savings into private pension funds is difficult to sustain initially.

- The envisaged structure and functions of private pension funds in Hungary and Poland. The comparative analysis shall focus on the details of the new schemes, the cost implications, consider the administrative norms and highlight the variety of side-effects emerging from the reform process.

- The opportunities for stock market development and pension fund asset managers. A shift away from an exclusive focus on state funded pension systems has a variety of indirect, longer-term side effects. It can enhance the creation of a new constituency of voters with a vested interest in sound economic policy-making. Inflation, which may matter less to the elderly receiving index-linked state pensions, is a threat to those whose present contributions and future retirement income depends upon the value of investments they have transferred into private schemes.

When policy-makers address the need to rebuild social insurance, they are thus embarking on a political minefield in post-communist societies. All countries in Central and Eastern Europe maintain statutory basic pension provisions through which the state guarantees a pension to everybody subject to the scheme. These pay-as-you-go pension schemes were an integral part of the *cradle-to-grave protection* afforded by socialist regimes until 1990. They are now proving a liability and are causing structural problems during the transition process. Central and East European economies are therefore faced with a number of structural features which deserve closer attention:

- The rapid *demographic transition*, resulting in an (i) increasing ratio of older to younger persons, as well as (ii) a shrinking labor force, and (iii) a shrinking birth rate. This ratio is expected to increase even further in the future. In Poland for instance, the *old age dependency ratio*[1] is forecast to increase by 50 percent within the coming 25 years.

- A rapidly rising share of pensioners is characteristic for Central and Eastern Europe. In *Hungary*, for instance, there is one pensioner for every five people of working age. Pensioners numbered over 3 million in January 1997, 30 percent of the population of 10.2 million. Again demographic forecasts paint a challenging picture. The future relationship between the number of contributors to the number of people receiving benefits from the social insurance system does not look optimistic. In Hungary the ratio is set to decrease from 2.1 in 1990 to 1.78 in 2020. In other words, the *system dependency rate* is increasing to alarming levels.

- A large percentage of voters in transition countries are pensioners who have repeatedly expressed a preference for voting with their pocketbooks.[2] To illustrate, in *Bulgaria* pensioners account for 25 percent of eligible voters, and the relative number of people receiving different kinds of pensions in Poland exceeded 40 percent at the beginning of 1997 (see table 10 next page).[3]

Central and East European countries are thus characterized by upward pressure on pension costs relative to GDP. If left unchecked, such pay-as-you-go pension systems will require an ever-growing fiscal burden, and risk to sink transition economies into chronic resource problems. In 1996 the Hungarian pension system had a deficit of $262 million, and this year's shortfall will exceed the optimistic $96 million deficit estimated in the 1997 budget. Hungary's overall social security deficit (health and pensions) ballooned to £250 million in 1996, four times the annual target. Next to the demographic burden another indicator speaks volumes of the exiting problems and challenges ahead: public pension spending as a share of GDP. *Poland* currently has 9 million pensioners (24 percent of its population) who receive 16 percent of GDP in benefits, one of the highest ratios in Europe, East and West! The social

Table 10
Basic social indicators of transition economies

1997	Population (millions)	Pensioners (millions)	Life expectancy (years)	Labor Force Age 15-64 (millions)	Unemployment	Pension Funds	Pension Expend. 1996*
Bulgaria	8.4	2.5	71	6	11.3	n.a.	9.2
Romania	22.7	5.2	70	15	9.2	n.a.	7.1
Poland	38.5	8.8	72	25	14.9	Plan	15.8
Hungary	10.3	3.1	70	7	10.4	212	10.3
Czech Republic	10.3	2.2	73	7	2.9	44	9.4
Slovakia	5.3	1.2	72	4	13.1	Plan	10.6
Estonia	1.5	206.000#	70	1	5.0	Plan	7.2
Lithuania	2.2	640.000#	71	900.000#	8.7	Plan	18.9

*   In percent of GDP.

Reference point is hundred thousand, not million.

Source: World Development Report (1996), EBRD (1997).

security system shortfall absorbed 14 percent of government expenditure in 1997. In the *Czech Republic* pension costs swallowed 27 percent of budget expenditure in 1996. Without a wholesale overhaul, the burden will grow even bigger in the foreseeable future (see table 11 next page).

The main reason for such high public spending ratios is the continuation of pay-as-you-go pension systems created in former communist countries in the late seventies, early eighties. Minimal changes have been introduced during the initial transition period between 1990-1997. The key deficits in the present systems are:

- The indexation of benefits, generally based on the rate of wage increases;

- During the old system many branches in the socialized sectors of the economy introduced special pension privileges for different occupational groups, for instance miners and military personnel;

- The introduction of numerous, and rather generous, early retirement schemes (often in conjunction with disability benefits) as a means of social policy-making in the early nineties;

- The high level of mandatory social insurance contributions causes many employers and employees to seek means and ways of reducing their spending to the system. This situation of avoidance strategies results in a continued importance of the gray zone in transition economies of Central and Eastern Europe. To illustrate: social security contributions levied on the 800,000 self-employed in Hungary were sharply increased in 1997. The payroll tax rates amounted to 45 percent of an individual's income on a monthly basis. The minimum contribution of Forint 7.650 (£27) is a serious sum when take-home pay is typically £122. The adverse effect of exorbitant non-wage burdens is twofold: (i) enterprises curtail full-time employment, and (ii) in order to avoid payment many self-employed switch to work in the hidden/informal economy. The

Constitutional Court in Hungary has been asked for a ruling on the issue.

Table 11
Pension provisions in Central and Eastern Europe

1996	Retirement Age		Pension	Coverage (% of Salary)
	Women	Men	Employee	Employer
Poland	60	65	7.2	26.8
Hungary	55	60	6.0	24.5
Czech Republic*	53-57	60	6.5	19.5
Slovakia*	53-57	60	5.9	21.6

* According to number of children raised in former Czechoslovakia.

Recent reforms in Hungary and Poland

It follows from these observations that introducing and sequencing pension reform in Central and Eastern Europe will demand *significant time resources* and *political determination* against vested interests. Pension funds are part and parcel of a market economy that takes considerable time to develop. Their close dependence on financial stability and on the emergence of institutions that bolster capital market efficiency account for the considered crafting of such reforms (EBRD 1997, p. 87). Moreover, reform initiatives will be judged by large segments of the citizenry in relation to their capacity to avoid, or curtail old-age poverty traps. More specifically, special attention needs to be given to those employed in the public sector whose basic pension provisions are often little above subsistence level. Large segments of public employees in Central and Eastern Europe have typically not been covered by designated occupational pension schemes. To date, the Hungarian and Polish governments are the two leading examples in Central and Eastern Europe where comprehensive reform initiatives have been submitted to the respective parliaments, and in the former case also become law.

Hungary

In *Hungary* parliament adopted three statutes in July 1997 on social welfare provision and pension funding (Laws LXXX to LXXXII 1997). The reforms will change the country's pension system in a way that seeks to enhance the nation's growing capital markets, and save the current pay-as-you-go system from eminent bankruptcy. To illustrate: according to the statistical office the total number of employees declined from 5.5 million in the year 1990 to barely 4 million in 1997 (data as of January respectively). During this period the number of pensioners rose from 2.6 million to slightly over 3 million. Unemployment rose from 24,000 to roughly 500,000. At present Hungary uses 10 percent of its GDP for old-age welfare. The new legislation makes Hungary the first of the former communist countries to comprehensively reform its pension system, and the second European nation after Switzerland to have a *mandatory* private pension scheme. The legislation has taken effect on January 1, 1998.

The traditional 'contract between generations' is based on Hungarians contributing 6 percent of their salaries, and employers putting an amount equal to 24 percent of workers pay into state-run pension funds. The new legislation reduces the employers' contribution to the *first pillar* by two percent in the year 2000, while the employees' share increases by one percent. Between the years 1998 and 2000 employers will contribute 15 percent of gross salary to compulsory health insurance and employees' share will be 3 percent. Employers paying a further 24 percent to state pension funds will see this percentage fall to 23 percent in 1999 and 22 percent in 2000. By contrast, Employees *not* participating in private pension funds (PPFs) will contribute 7 percent of gross wages to the state pension scheme in 1998. This will rise by one basis point per year, reaching 9 percent in 2000. This *first pillar* still accounts for over 75 percent of all old-age insurance in Hungary. At the beginning of 1996 the Horn government passed a first pension reform bill which increased the statutory pension age from currently 55 for women and 60 for men to a unified 62 years.

From 1998 onwards, Hungarians aged 62 years and older, who have 20 years of employment and contributions, qualify for the basic state pension within the first pillar. Ten years of pensionable employment secures a pension of 33 percent of the last average monthly wage, while 40 years of employment yields a pension of 80 percent (Falush 1997).

Since 1993 Hungarians also have the legal option of a *third pillar*. Such private pension and life insurance options are based on voluntary, supplementary contributions. The so-called *Voluntary Mutual Benefit Funds* (VMBFs) were established by Law XCVI in 1993. They are tax-advantaged providers of third-tier pensions. To date 250 such funds exist. VMBFs are said to have attracted an estimated 800,000 pension contributors by the end of 1997. While this number is not inconsiderable, and rising, it can nevertheless be argued that the VMBFs have not made the kind of progress initially hoped-for. The low participation rate is strongly shaped by the aforementioned high level of social security contributions that Hungarian employees have to muster. Consequently, middle and low-income groups hardly have any incentives to participate in a third pillar that further squeezes their disposable income if they were to sign-up for VMBFs. In order to enhance the take-up rate the new legislation proposes various schemes to give tax credits to those who subscribe to the third pillar.

The new system establishes a bridge from the existing single pillar system to a three-tier pension architecture under which Hungarians' contributions to their retirement accounts will also go into privately run, mandatory funds. The introduction of an *obligatory second pillar* is financed by capitalization. Employees becoming a member of PPFs in 1998 will contribute 1 percent of their gross wages to the state pension fund and 6 percent to the new scheme. By the year 2000 the contributions to such new private pension funds are planed to rise to eight percent of Hungarians' salaries. The total employee contribution to PPFs may reach a ceiling of 10 percent of gross wages. The 1998 budget includes a provision that employee contributions in excess of 6 percent are tax deductible at a rate of 25 percent of personal income tax (PIT). All new entrants into the workforce from 30.6.1998 onwards, who are below 42 years of age, will be required to participate in the new second pillar. They can choose which PPF they wish to subscribe to. Those already in employment who are 47 years old or younger will be able to choose whether or not they which to join a PPF. People older than 47 will *not* be able to opt out of the current system. As a means of partial compensation, the state will guarantee those between 42 and 47 years of age that their private pension will equal at least 25 percent of the state pension on the day of their retirement. Periods of unemployment and illness will not serve to reduce the minimum threshold of 180 months of contributions into a PPF. Pensions from individual retirement account of the second pillar will be eligible after 180 monthly contributions have been made. Until the year 2013 pension payments are not subject to PIT. According to Reed (1998) since the privatization programme started in 1998, upward of 800,000 Hungarians have switched from the state-run system to the mixed plan.

Authorization and supervision of private pension funds is established by *Allami Pénztárfelügyelet* (State Pension Fund Supervision, SPFS). The national PPFs authority will monitor target rates of return on investments, issue licenses for the creation of new private funds, and regulate cross-ownership with foreign institutional investors. By the end of 1997 a total of 48 PPFs had been licensed, some as newly established entities, others through a conversion from existing VMBFs in the third pillar. The largest PPFs are *AB-Aegon* with 34,000 members, the Austrian insurance company *Winterthur* with 26,000 members and the Dutch *ABN-AMRO* registering 21,000 members. Further regulations include a 10 percent limit on investments in one security, PPFs investment in equities, real estate and mortgages is limited to 60 percent. Before the turn of the century foreign securities may not be held, but 30 percent are possible by 2002 (with at least 70 percent of the total held in OECD country securities). PPFs may not own derivatives, except for hedging purposes.

Significantly, the need for pension reform was accepted by the *National Confederation of Hungarian Trade Unions*, an interest organization representing 48 unions with over 800,000 members. However, they succeeded in receiving concessions. The confederation pushed to have employees' contributions to the private funds lowered from the 10 percent provided for in an earlier version of the bill, and to institute a performance guarantee for the funds. The setting of such a performance guarantee remains a bone of contention in the negotiations. Finally, it is noteworthy that the Hungarian reform efforts have also received critical support from international financial institutions such as the *World Bank*. In January 1998 the Bank approved a $150 million loan to support the Horn government's determination to implement pension system reform. A representative from the *World Bank*, Jean-Jacques Dethier, claimed,

> This is the first comprehensive pension reform in Central and Eastern Europe, and it will set the standards for the other transition economies. It represents a major improvement over the previous systems and should protect pensioners while greatly improving fiscal accounts (Reuters 28 January 1998).

After almost one year in operation, pension-fund management remains a high-risk endeavour for the government, banks and insurance companies alike. With the number of people switching over to the new plan soon to reach the one-million threshold, Hungary's old system will face a deficit of some 20 billion forints ($95 million) in 1998. Furthermore, seen through the lens of institutional actors, the programme's barriers to entry are rather low. Would-be pension fund managers can establish themselves with as few as 2,000 participants. For institutions seeking to attract big client volumes, this threshold requirement risks to inflate the number of competitors and fragments the overall enterprise. At present (June 1998), a variety of big international funds managed by *Dutch Aegon NV, ING Grop NV's Nationale-Nederlanden*, and *Credit Suisse's Winterthur Insurance Co.* are among the larger players. But more than 50 smaller, predominantly domestic, funds have mushroomed in the course of the year. This explosion in numbers alongside a discrepancy between large [foreign] institutional operators and rather small niche players will require some form of consolidation in the coming years. In all likelihood a flurry of fund mergers and acquisitions will have to take place, but possibly some bankruptcies cannot be excluded.

Poland

In *Poland*, the new center-right government, in office since October 1997, is to press ahead with plans inherited from the former SLD/PSL administration of Prime Minister Wlodzimierz Cimoszewicz to reform the current system of funding pensions with payroll taxes.[4] The initial reform plans have been modified by the new *AWS/Freedom Union* coalition government of Prime Minister Jerzy Buzek. With the help of the *World Bank*, which is backing the project through funds and loans, the new deputy Prime Minister in charge of the economy, Leszek Balcerowicz, wants introduce privately managed pension funds at the beginning of 1999. The aim is to switch people gradually into a private system by adding two new layers of investment-funded pensions. For people in employment under the age of 30, the private pension funds will be compulsory. These will supplement a basic state pension, funded on traditional pay-as-you-go schemes, as well as voluntary private pension plans. Ewa Lewicka, deputy Labor Minister in charge of the reforms, regards the reform initiative as crucial to increasing the rate of savings in the economy. Introducing the new system by January 1, 1999 would require the passage of extensive legislation tightening the system of pensions paid to the elderly and those receiving disability benefits.

However, there is a considerable price tag attached to this programme. The proposals seek to index funded pensions to the combined growth of wages and employment. In practice such a design would turn out to be a fiendishly expensive formula. Currently, the growth of pension income is pegged to the consumer price index (standing at 16.8 percent in April 1998), while in 1992 it was linked to average wage rises. Still, Balcerowicz' objective to balance public sector finances by 2003, a goal that is contained in the minister's medium-term financial strategy running until 2001, the next parliamentary election year, will further affect the timing as well as the scope and content of the planed health service reforms. More specifically, there is a risk that these reforms may be stalled because of Mr Balcerowicz' warnings that - at present - the costs would amount to 9.8bn Zlotys a year to implement (equivalent to 1.5 percent of GDP).

The reform proposals are currently subject to scrutiny in parliamentary committees following revisions, which Balcerowicz submitted at the beginning of 1998. Apart from establishing private pension funds, other legislative drafts seek to reorganize the resource basis of the first pillar by planing to use the proceeds from a new round of mass privatizations of state-owned firms to finance the reform package. Such privatizations are due to take place *before* the pension reforms are to be implemented. The revenue earmarked for the later reform will be retained in the form of issuing convertible bonds, which will subsequently be redeemed into shares of privatized companies. This means of finance is subject to considerable criticism in the parliamentary committees. It is not yet clear which firms would be involved, and how intra-ministerial decision making between the Treasury and the Labor department is to proceed.[5]

The current single-pillar pension system dates back to the communist era. The pay-as-you-go model implies that employers transfer mandatory social security contributions to the *Social Insurance Office* (ZUS, presided over by Stanislaw Alot since January 1998), the sole state pension provider in Poland. These transfers total 45 percent of workers' gross income. Subsequently, the ZUS pays pensioners from current income *and* subsidies from the central budget. The latter accounted for 16 percent of budget spending in 1996. Under the reforms, the Buzek government intends to cut the social security charge of 45 percent on gross wages to 35 percent over 15 years, and thereafter to a "target of 30 percent" (Lewicka, quoted in Reuters 1997). As mentioned, the charge is currently paid by employers, but the reforms provide for a split between employers and employees, easing employers' wage bills in the medium term.

Let us look more specifically at the architecture of pension reform in Poland. The future pension system should be composed of three pillars. The *first pillar* remains mandatory with payments to ZUS at four-fifths of the current level, evenly divided between employers and employees. These contributions will pay a "minimum" pension, which is guaranteed by the state. The *second pillar* is equally obligatory, but is based on the defined contribution system of privately managed pension funds. The government is planing a system of 10-20 private pension funds with individual retirement accounts. The new funds would receive 20 percent of mandatory premiums currently paid into the ZUS, thereby constituting the remaining fifth of present compulsory ZUS contributions. Of the 45 percent of salaries currently contributed to the social security system, an absolute 9 percent would be channeled into the second pillar. People under the age of 30 years would be obliged to join, while others could become voluntary members. The *third pillar* will involve people voluntarily topping up their benefits through employer-sponsored corporate pension funds, insurance or other investment schemes. Further details include:

- The privately run pension fund management companies would require a 51 percent ownership structure held by a Polish firm. According to the law firm of *Cameron McKenna* (one of many Western architects of the Polish reform) the second pillar should reach a capitalization of $1.5 billion by the end of 1999.

- According to the Finance Ministry the start-up costs to a multi-pillar model are estimated to amount to 4.4 percent of GDP in the first year. The ensuing debt could reach 15.3 percent of GDP in 2002.

- The anticipated pension reforms in Poland have not gone unnoticed among foreign institutional investors. In January 1998 *DWS Polska TFP S.A. Grupa Deutsche Bank* (Deutsche Gesellschaft für Wertpapiersparen m.b.H.) was launched in Warsaw. Majority owned by *Deutsche Bank* (93 percent), *DWS Polska* will offer four different funds: (i) mixed funds, (ii) equity funds, (iii) privatization funds, and (iv) private pension funds.

Does Chile provide lessons for pension reform?

The development of *private pension* institutions and life insurance companies - and thus a general reduction in the reliance on pay-as-you-go financing of social security - represents a key factor in the *future performance of emerging markets* for raising savings rates, boost investment and spur economic growth. As Central and Eastern European countries reform their general basic pension systems in response to demographic trends and state budget concerns, they will need to develop specialized pension schemes for different occupational groups, including civil servants.

In preparing pension reforms, comparative experiences from other countries and regions can help to clarify national needs, and highlight possible strategies related to the introduction of private pension funds. Since there does not exist a ready-made blueprint, Central and Eastern European countries are attracted by the success of Latin American examples, in particular Chile's reform process. The Polish pension reform proposals have been classified as being "very similar to the Chilean model" (Pater 1997). What could they learn from such a country? Almost twenty years ago, in 1981, Chile privatized its pension system, introducing heavily regulated pension funds. This pioneering reform is claimed to have underpinned the country's spectacular rise in its national savings rate, from 8.2 percent of GDP in 1981 to 27.6 percent in 1995. The purpose of Chile's reform was to replace a near-bankrupt public pension system with one based on individual retirement accounts. Workers were required to provide for their own retirement by putting at least 13 percent of their salaries into privately managed - but closely regulated - pension funds.[6] They are free to choose among competing fund managers. The *defined contribution system* of Chile implies that the state guarantees only a minimum benefit as a safety net.[7] What presumed *advantages* would a shift to a fully funded private pension system thus yield in Central and Eastern European countries?

- On the most general level it would prevent governments penalizing future generations through their generosity to current ones. In other words, pensions would cease to be an exclusive government issue.

- Savings rates may rise if the minimum contribution an employee/worker must make to his/her pension fund is more than he would voluntarily save, or if the higher returns earned by these funds prompt him to save more. However, one should not ignore the direct loss of savings due to private pension reform. This includes the public spending involved in providing pensions to people who retired under the old system, as the government no longer receives new contributions from current workers to pay pensioners. Additional costs accrue by the need to compensate workers who switched to private funds for the payments they had previously made into the old system. In short, the overall direct impact of pension funds on saving may *initially* be negative.[8]

- The emerging financial sector in transition countries may benefit as competition between pension funds creates more efficient capital markets. Hence stock market capitalization as a percentage of GDP may increase (considerably). Furthermore, the development of an active long-term corporate-bond market constitutes a welcome by-product. In *Hungary* experts expect that some of the money in the emerging private funds will be invested in the Budapest Stock Exchange, helping to develop the market and lessen its reliance on globe-hopping foreign capital. It is estimated that $1 billion will go into the new funds (Agovino 1997).

- Labor market distortions, in particular in the (formerly) socialized sector of the economy, may be reduced. Whereas a pay-as-you-go system encourages employers to hire 'informal' or unregistered workers to avoid paying the payroll tax, a private system gives workers an incentive to work on the books so they can contribute to their own retirement accounts. By the same token, employment mobility is improved.

Such advantages have been phrased in a cautious manner. The reason for this hesitance lies in the argument that correlation does not prove causation, neither in the present case of Chile's private pension reform, nor in the future initiatives in Central and Eastern Europe. Almost a decade into their respective transition processes, the latter countries are still operating under conditions of a turbulent environment, as experienced in the Summer 1997 floods in Poland or the currency crisis in Spring 1997 in the Czech Republic. Furthermore, while pension reform is a central element in the consolidation of the transformation process, it is all the more difficult to identify how much pension reform is/was responsible for transition. In other words, introducing a private pension system in Poland, Hungary or the Czech Republic may prove beneficial, but for other reasons than many of their avid protagonists claim:

- Questions remain about whether a programme devised for a young population in a developing country is suitable for older societies in Central and Eastern Europe. Equally, the system's high administrative costs cannot be underestimated in transition countries whose administrative performance is itself subject to profound change.

- The growth of pension funds can have a positive effect for the development of financial markets in transition countries. If legislation provides for private pension funds to invest into equities, the stock market index will rise. The example of Chile illustrates that trading in stocks and bonds grew in line with pension-fund assets, suggesting that the funds became a big source of market liquidity. What is less clear is the degree to which the funds account for a proportion of total share holdings.

- The aforementioned positive savings effect through the introduction of private pension schemes in Central and Eastern Europe can rather be indirect, but still beneficial. The transition costs to a new retirement system will possibly require cutting public expenditure. Stringent fiscal policies raise the savings rate directly because the public sector's surplus or deficit is a core ingredient of national saving.

- Consolidated and more liquid capital markets add to the efficiency effect with which savings are used. Against the background of transitional fiscal costs associated with privatizing pension funds, the government's determination to tighten its budget belt through sound fiscal policy is a major parameter in this process.

- The regulatory framework and administration of pension funds is hardly comparable between Chile and transition countries. In the latter set of countries the reform steps undertaken require an administrative underpinning which is yet to be fully implemented, let alone consolidated. To illustrate: the administration of pensions depends *inter alia* on (i) collecting and registering data on pensionable earnings, (ii) regulating and fixing benefits, (iii) managing the pension capital, (iv) external audit mechanisms etc. Such administrative details will vary considerably depending on (a) whether pension provisions are benefit- or contribution-defined, (b) whether benefits are based on final salary or career earnings, and (c) whether pre-funding finances them or pay-as-you go systems. Highlighting this administrative context serves the purpose to emphasize how much such an institutional architecture ensures legal certainty and equal treatment.[9] Both objectives are paramount in societies whose pace and scope of change in the past eight years has been breath-taking, and where citizens as well as financial institutions demand such predictability.

Questions still searching for answers

The fact that pension reform is starting to move up the agenda of public policy-making in Central and Eastern Europe is a reflection of new priorities in the transition process. While macro-economic privatization of state-owned firms is making significant progress, attention is gradually being switched to micro-economic issues. One such area concerns social-security privatization. More specifically, pension reform is identified as a major means to ease the state's fiscal burden and empower citizens to seize greater control of their economic future. The process of social insurance reform in Central and Eastern Europe involves balancing the often-conflicting interests of government, business and citizens. Careful, concise legislation is a further indispensable pre-condition. Summing up, the following observations ought to be of interest in a comparative perspective:

- The reform of social insurance systems in Central and Eastern Europe - in particular pension reform - is rapidly gaining currency.

In virtually every country of Central and Eastern Europe the debate rages on and legislation is being tabled to parliament. The objective consists in establishing a new system of public and private partnership in pensions. State provisions in transition countries of Central and Eastern Europe are expensive and have been ill-designed to cope with high rates of inflation during the transformation process. Overall, since 1989/90 public pension systems have delivered a rising degree of income inequality in retirement. Pay-as-you-go schemes have thus come under considerable pressure for change. The initial political constituency for change came as a result of fiscal crises, which transition economies are currently undergoing. However, while such a shift may alleviate public finances in the short term, it is increasingly questionable whether countries in Central and Eastern Europe can save their way out of demographic problems.

- The core challenge thus consists in sustaining the confidence of the public in the state pension system while introducing private multi-pillar pension schemes. The turbulent environment, which so characterizes the magnitude of change in Central and Eastern Europe, makes the task of fostering a proper public debate about pension reform difficult and ambiguous, but no less critical. The complexity of the task, its legislative requirements, institutional preconditions and normative aspects such as the principle of social solidarity further compound the endeavor.

- The urgency for pension reform is underlined, and closely monitored, by international organizations such as the EBRD, the World Bank, the IMF and the European Commission.[10] Governments in Hungary and Poland have passed or submitted to parliament detailed plans to introduce private pension systems, which supplement the existing architecture of old age social security.[11] The solution devised seeks to reduce the role of the state scheme to that of a poverty-alleviating mechanism. Moreover, although most countries in Central and Eastern Europe have, for economic as well as for social reasons, implemented early retirement schemes during the past seven years, there has recently been a change in policy priorities towards reversing this trend. Another feature of recent developments consists in raising the age of retirement, as exemplified by Hungary.

- Prevailing demographic changes are the most important, but not the sole reason obliging post-communist countries to implement changes in the existing social insurance systems. The share of public pension spending in the GDP is high, if not extremely high in transition countries, thus forcing policy adjustments and wholesale reform at the earliest possible stage. However, one of the main difficulties will be finding a way to finance the costs of transition to multi-tier pension systems without causing inflationary effects. Contributions into the PAYG schemes decline as soon as the privatized pension reform is initiated. But the benefits paid from the existing state schemes remain considerable as a proportion of social insurance expenditure for at least 10 to 15 years before the new first pillar eventually breaks even. Such transition costs may have a positive side-effect: obliging countries to reshape, *inter alia*, their fiscal policies by putting a tight lid on public expenditure. Equally, the cost dimension will contribute to increase the public and private sectors' efficiency with which savings are used.

- The importance of pension reform in Central and Eastern Europe reaches beyond the obvious public expenditure implications. The reform process is also a cornerstone in the drive to overcome paternalism and encourage more self-responsibility. Equally, the creation of institutional investors energizes emerging capital markets, in particular the much-needed capitalization of the respective stock exchanges. The inter-relation between privatization and pension fund reform should also not be underestimated. To illustrate: the government of Croatia began the sale of a final stake in *Pliva*, Eastern Europe's biggest pharmaceutical company, in April 1998. The government sold its remaining 14 percent stake, following the company's initial public offering in early 1996. The international offering is the country's biggest privatization to date, increasing the free float of *Pliva* shares to 54.5 percent. The state no longer holds shares directly, although various public pension funds and Croatian banks retain holdings of 45.5 percent.

- Furthermore, setting up a supplementary 2nd pillar financed by capitalization advances the willingness of employees and enterprise for the long-term volume of national savings and investment. The potential is enormous. If the Chilean experience can serve as an approximation, then at least 1/3 of the present contributions in a country like Poland can be directed to private pension funds within the first five years of operation.

- Both in Hungary and Poland, the introduction of private pension funds includes a mixture of 'carrot and stick'. Specific age groups of the active labor force are obliged to start making savings of their salary in private funds. This raises the dual question of how compelling it is to make such savings obligatory, and where the threshold should be set? Arguably, there is a case that people should be made to save something for old age. But how much? Requiring people to save a share of their incomes in addition to contributing to the basic state pension can lead governments trying to force workers to save excessively. In New Zealand, for instance, 92 percent voted against compulsory pensions in a referendum in September 1997 (The Economist 1998, p. 74). It is far from clear how much saving is legitimate to require. Peoples' preferred retirement income and preferences differ over time and across occupational groups (Jupp 1998). Furthermore, any stated link between compulsory savings serving to boost national saving, thus leading to higher investments and faster growth, are far from evident. Since state pension schemes are being scaled back in Central and Eastern Europe, some degree of compulsion may be needed to prevent people ending up a burden on taxpayers. But beyond the necessary definition of what constitutes a minimum, second-guessing individuals' savings decisions is hard to justify, all the more in post-communist societies whose populations have endured more than 40 years of government intrusion in peoples' lives.

- Given the magnitude of change which the populations in Central and Eastern Europe have experienced since 1989/90, it may *not* take a generation for these societies to abandon their reservations about fund-based pensions. When analyzing various concepts about pension reform in Central and Eastern Europe, a basic, initial question must be answered: What should be the role of pension funds in the future social insurance architecture of these countries – should they be voluntary or mandatory? In light of the examples presented from Hungary and Poland, the likely answer will be "mandatory". However, the flip-side of this argument is a high degree of individual choice in other areas. To illustrate: Hungary's new pension scheme allows individuals to switch pension-fund companies as often as every six months. The idea to maximize choice may be attractive for prospective clients. But fund managers, who face steep initial costs when recruiting such clients, may subsequently think twice about the fundamentals of the pension business in Hungary.

- With the advent of the pension fund a catalyst is energized in transition countries. Emerging markets in Central and Eastern Europe are gearing up for forthcoming changes in the architecture of pension regulation. The recognition by political parties that reform is urgently needed feeds into the interest shown by domestic and foreign banks, insurance companies and institutional funds to investment considerable resources. The *Pioneer First Polish Trust Fund Company, American International Group, ING Barings*, and *Allianz AG*[12] are among international finance and insurance companies competing for licenses once private pension funds are established. They are seeking to expand into new markets whose demand for modern risk management is growing the more economic transition is consolidated. However, the major bone of contention remains the reluctance of government regulators in Poland and Hungary to allow such foreign financial institutions to have a majority portfolio in the new funds. Regulating market entry by foreign providers remains a delicate matter.

- The institutional architecture of private pension funds in Central and Eastern European countries needs to be clarified further. Given that capital markets in Central and Eastern Europe are still rather unsophisticated and financial operators have little experience in pension portfolio management, attention to detail is paramount. Thus, tight regulation of pension funds are initially unavoidable, even if such regulatory straitjackets yield sub-optimal returns. Further questions searching for answers concern: (i) The mix between profit and non-profit companies managing pension funds; (ii) The future role played by banks, insurance companies and other financial institutions as shareholders in pension funds; (iii) Can individual persons become shareholders? (iv) How is cross-ownership in different pension funds regulated, i.e. limited? (v) What is the level of required diversification in a pension fund's portfolio, e.g. what degree of a fund's assets can be invested in securities guaranteed by the respective central banks, or in companies listed on the stock exchanges?

- The current debate on rebuilding social insurance in post-communist countries is timely and critical to the performance of the transition process. Demonstrating the benefits of funded, personal, basic pensions is an endeavor that will require considerable political will and endurance. In order to make this undertaking commercially deliverable and publicly acceptable key aspects deserve further elaboration: (i) The government's role as *organizer, regulator* and *guarantor* of basic pensions, but not necessarily as the *provider* of services; (ii) The future scope and character of a *basic pension* in transition economies; (iii) The *regulatory framework* that focuses on providers and products; (iv) The incentives, distribution channels and the administrative architecture needed to implement and service private pension funds.

- Can we thus call 'three cheers for pension reform' in Central and Eastern Europe? Not yet, nor unconditionally. Establishing a culture of private provision for old-age income in Central and Eastern Europe will take time and consistency. Governments have an important regulatory role to play, with a cautious approach, rather than a 'quick fix' of the pension system, being the order of the day. Within this framework, every country will have some strategic choices to make about the relative size of the three pillars and the specific design of each. The precise choice depends on a country's objectives and its constraints. The legislation adopted in Hungary and proposed in Poland underlines that the reforms will change the basic nature of mandatory pension provision by placing a large(r) share on a fully-funded, and privately managed, basis with individual retirement accounts. Through the comparative perspective post-communist countries are learning from other experiments, and are considering the options for importing pension reform initiatives. In this context the approach of *European Union* member countries to social security reforms, and the experience of Central and Eastern Europe when introducing private pension funds may prove mutually beneficial. It thus suffices to conclude that eight years into their transition from plan to market such a statement about post-communist societies is remarkable in itself.

Notes

1   The old age dependency ratio refers to the number of men and women over 64 and 69 respectively, divided by the number of men and women aged 18 to 64 and 18 to 69 respectively.

2   During the September 1997 general elections in Poland, the *Pensioners' Party* (KPEiR) ran for parliamentary representation. The KPEiR failed to clear the 5 percent voting threshold, receiving 3.7 percent. But the party's performance underlined that vested interests of pensioners are a force to be reckoned with in Polish politics. In the Czech Republic, a new party, the *Pensioners for a Secure Life* (DZJ), is running for the general elections in June 1998. The pensioners' party claims to have 55,000 members organized in over 500 local groups. If these figures are correct, the DJZ would have the largest membership base among all Czech parties. Led by 68-year-old Eduard Kremlicka, a former career army officer and long-time member of the Communist Party, the

DZJ is campaigning on a platform of increased pensions for the elderly and slower price liberalization for housing, electricity and public transport. There are over 2.2 million pensioners in the Czech Republic, who represent almost one-fourth of the population and one-third of the electorate. Pensioners in the Czech Republic have hardly benefited from the economic transition process. Their real income is still 10 percent below the level of 1989. Two-thirds of the elderly have to make ends meet with a disposable income that lies *below* the average pension of 5,180 Czech Crones, corresponding to roughly £ 100 (Sterling).

3   At present an average Polish pension is 608 Zlotys (USD 200) a month, equalling roughly 60 percent of the average monthly wage. Pension arrears are not (yet) a problem in Poland, Hungary and the Czech Republic. However, they are a major challenge in Russia, where large monopolies such as *Gazprom* and *Unified Energy Systems*, as well as the *Railways Ministry* are the biggest offenders in pension arrears.

4   However, before the Cimoszewicz government left office in autumn 1997, parliament's lower house, the *Sejm*, had passed just three of the 11 projected laws needed to put the new pension system into effect. It is thus up to the successor government of Prime Minister Buzek to complete the unfinished business. The new government has announced to retain the reform legislation inherited from its predecessor. Yet, the task that still lies ahead is anything from self-evident. The new Prime Minister is in a so-called *cohabitation* arrangement with the Polish President, A. Kwasniewski. While the former has roots in the legendary *Solidarnosc* trade union, the latter was a Communist Party sports minister until mid-1989. The constitution gives the President a veto over all legislation except the annual budget. Presidential vetoes can, however, be overturned with the support of 60 percent of the deputies in the *Sejm*. The *AWS/Freedom Union* government coalition controls just under 60 percent of the seats in parliament's lower house. President Kwasniewski has shown that he can use these prerogatives effectively when he blocked government plans to cut *military pensions* in December 1997. As part of its comprehensive pension reform proposals, the Buzek government

had started to phase out special pension privileges won in the past by different categories of employees, particularly for farmers and the military. These privileges not only burden the social insurance budget, but also clash with the intentions of the new pension system that payments must reflect individual contributions. The Buzek government thus moved to scrap a provision where annual adjustments to military pensions are higher than for civilians, only to be called back by the President.

5   Using state assets to support the reform of the social insurance system implies that the process will have a significant impact on the future privatization in Poland. In other words, a host of sensitive decisions will have to be made about (i) the choice of assets, (ii) their valuation, (iii) their prospective profitability, and (iv) the amount which is channelled to the state budget. It is rather self-evident that such decisions will be controversial, subject to possible litigation, and thus highly politicised. In his inaugural policy declaration in November 1997, the new Polish Prime Minister, Jerzy Buzek (AWS), has maintained his predecessors approach to combine the reform of the pension system with the ongoing mass privatization process.

6   The reform is a lasting legacy of the former Chilean dictator, General Augusto Pinochet. Ironically, the police and armed forces were exempted from the reform.

7   Public pension schemes in Central and Eastern Europe are *defined benefit systems*.

8   According to *Fidler* (1997) pension provision is unsatisfactory. Only 60 percent of Chilean workers are in effect covered by the private system.

9   The so-called *SIGMA* programme (Support for Improvement in Governance and Management in Central and Eastern European Countries) is a joint initiative of the *OECD* and the European Union. *SIGMA* supports public administration reform efforts in thirteen countries in transition.

10   The *European Union* legislative context will become increasingly important during the association negotiations, which have started with the Czech Republic, Poland, Hungary, Slovenia and Estonia in the summer of 1997. Streamlining national social welfare policies

in the five candidate countries from Central and Eastern Europe will be paramount. One such area, for instance, concerns the recommendation from Brussels on the equalization of the retirement age for men and women.

11 Even the government of Kazakhstan launched a private pension reform at the beginning of 1998. Its PAYG system has accumulated more than $500 million in debt at the end of 1997, forcing a government bailout. The reform is backed by $400 million in loans from the *Asian Development Bank* and the *World Bank* (Benoit 1998).

12 In 1990 Germany's *Allianz* bought 49 percent of *Hungaria Biztosito*, one of the country's two state insurers. In April 1996 *Allianz/Hungaria* launched an occupational pension fund, which became a runaway success. So far it has attracted some 38,000 members and over 1 billion Forints of assets (The Economist 1997).

References

Agovino, Th. (1997), *Hungary: Bill Would Privatize Pensions*, International Herald Tribune, June 5, 1997.

Andrews, E. S. and Mansoora, R. (1996), *The Financing of Pension Systems in Central and Eastern Europe. An Overview of Major Trends and their Determinants, 1990-1993*, World Bank Technical Paper No. 339, Social Challenges of Transition Series, World Bank: Washington D.C.

Benoit, B. (1998), "What East Can Teach West About Pensions", in *The Wall Street Journal Europe*, 03 February 1998.

Centre for Social Policy (1996), *Transformation of the Pension System in the Slovak Republic*, National report for the international research project 'Transformation of Pension Systems in Central and Eastern Europe', Co-ordination by the Centre for Social Policy, University of Bremen, Germany.

EBRD = European Bank for Reconstruction and Development (1997), *Transition Report 1996. Infrastructure and Savings*, EBRD: London.

The Economist, October 4th 1997, *Management Brief. Central European Cover Story*, pp. 112-113.

----, April 11th 1998, *Compelling Reasons to Save*, p. 74.

East European Insurance Review (1997), *Hungary: The Market, New Private Pensions Regime*, EEIR - 085, pp. 13-16.

Eddy, K. (1998), 'Not-so-Bad' Factor Leaves Hungarian Voters Unmoved', *Financial Times*, 08.05.1998, p. 3.

European Commission (1997), *Pension Systems and Reforms - Britain, Hungary, Italy, Poland, and Sweden*, European Commission's Phare ACE Programme, Research Project P95-2139-R.

Falush, P. (1997), "Hungary: The Market, New Private Pensions Regime", *East European Insurance Review* 085, November 1997, pp. 13-16.

Fidler, St. (1997), *Lure of the Latin Model*, Financial Times, 09 April 1997.

Holzmann, R. (1996), *Pension Reform, Financial Market Development, and Economic Growth: Preliminary Evidence from Chile*, IMF Working Paper WP/96/94.

Jupp, B. (1998), *Reasonable Force: The Place of Compulsion in Securing Adequate Pensions*. London: Demos.

New Europe (1997), *Polish Parliament Debates Key Pension Reform Bills*, New Europe, No. 208, May 18-24, 1997.

Pater, K. (1997), *The Role of Pension Funds in the Future Pension System in Poland*, Ministry of Privatization.

Reed, J. (1998), *The Outlook: Hungary Offers Tips for Pension Reformers*, The Wall Street Journal of Europe, 25.05.1998, p. 1.

Reuters, 28 January 1998, *World Bank Approves $150 mln Loan to Hungary*.

Sachs, J. and Warner, A. (1996), *Achieving Rapid Growth in the Transition Economies of Central Europe*, HIID Development Discussion Paper No. 544, July 1996.

5 The development of independent media in Central and Eastern Europe

Nadja Hahn

Introduction

> It is said that the press is a seventh superpower. I don't know which superpower it is, but it is definitely a superpower. It carries a great deal of responsibility for our common fate, for what we know and what we don't, what we should worry about and what we shouldn't, what we should believe in and what we should not. In it's own way, the press - as a part of the information and communication system of today's civilization - is a soul of the soul of all kind. It is a meaning of self-understanding (Havel 1995).

President Vaclav Havel of the Czech Republic delivered these remarks in 1992. The reforms towards a democratic and capitalist society had already entered their third year. At this time, 'media wars' and media privatization made daily headlines within and outside of Central and Eastern Europe. Domestically, electronic media became the object of political battles between the branches of governments, while the printed press faced not only severe economic problems, but also struggled for editorial independence from its owners. Internationally, observers were increasingly concerned with the implications of the often unbridled media developments for the future democratization and economic performance of transition countries. While the legislative and regulatory framework is still in the making, the media finds itself being the very subject of transition.

The degree of media independence is taken as an indicator which informs us about the nature of the political economy of transition in CEE. Its determinants reflect the unique challenge of moving simultaneously towards democracy and a free market economy. Breaking up the communist media - with its legend as a state-owned propaganda mouth-piece of the ruling élite - requires political action in terms of de-regulation, as well as the privatization of media and media-related businesses. Consequently, the two biggest obstacles on the way towards an independent media are government control over television and broadcasting, and economic problems facing the printed press. The first years of transition reveal an increasingly independent printed press, whereas the electronic media remains firmly in the hands of most governments. This paper will analyze both developments, with emphasis on the persistence of government control.

Section 1 will provide the theoretical background of media politics in transition countries. The analysis will draw attention to remaining communist legacies, discuss the media's relevance for democracy, as well as outline determinants of media independence. Section 2 investigates the economic dilemma of the printed press, including the persistence of state monopolies in print and distribution facilities. Here, the focus will be on the de-monopolization of ownership. Section 3 discusses the political battles over the de-regulation of TV and broadcasting. It will stress the so-called 'media wars' fought over new media legislation, specifically dismantling state dominance in management positions. The section equally highlights the potential censorship inherent in newly passed libel legislation, ending with a discussion about future media regulation. The conclusions underline the hypothesis that the struggle towards media independence is closely correlated to the success of the reform process, illustrating the general persistence of Communist ways of steering politics and business in transition countries. The need for foreign investment in the media and increasing international pressure are recognized as avenues out of governments' claws.

The term *media* will be interpreted as TV and broadcasting on the one hand, and the printed press, on the other - excluding all other forms of mass communication. Selected case studies are chosen to provide an overview of different developments. Hence the analysis is biased in favor of highlighting specific issues, rather than providing a coherent comparison between countries.[1]

Media in transition

Communist legacies

Under communism the media functioned as a propaganda tool, seeking to control all flows of information, thereby enabling ruling élites to successfully engage in "cultural policy". A high density of televisions and radios ensured "thought control" and the "indoctrination of the fundamental tenets of socialism: social equality and social ownership of the means of production" (Jakubowicz 1994a, p. 275). The governments' control tools included financial and administrative means, top management appointments, allocation of frequencies and newsprint, monopolies of press distribution, pre-publication censorship, banning international information flows, etc. (Jakubowicz 1995a, p. 127).

With the development of dissident movements, as well as the rise of the 'second economy', the print media began to liberalize slowly in the 1970's. During the 1980's, the electronic media also opened up, and more and more Western popular culture programmes were broadcast. In addition, satellite technology allowed airwaves from the West to be received in most Central European countries, further undermining the Communist monopoly on information (Splichal 1994, p. 28). The silent 'media revolution' therefore received recognition as one of the prime actors in the overthrow of Communist regimes. «While the revolutions of 1989 were seen as a victory for liberal values over authoritarianism, in subsequent years it has become clear that the absence of communism does not alone lead to democracy by default» (O'Neil 1996, p. 1). Remaining legacies of the communist regimes represent significant obstacles to the development of independent media. They can be classified into four groups:

Historical legacies: whether countries can refer to democratic experience, most notably in the inter-war period, and to what degree different regimes controlled the media under communism.

Constitutional legacies: in all transition countries initial media reform occurred in a legal and regulatory vacuum. This was either due to inadequate Communist media legislation, which was simply amended, or to new, but vaguely formulated laws. Developments strongly depended on whether or not the countries amended their old constitutions or created new ones.

Economic legacies: these refer to the difficulties of breaking up communist press-, print-, and distribution monopolies, all of which were directly controlled by Communist Party organizations and trade unions. In addition, alternative financial sources have to be found in order to replace government subsidies.

Ideological legacies: these concern attitudes towards journalism in terms of (i) professionalism, objectivity, methods of investigation by journalists, and (ii) attitudes of the public and government towards journalism (Jakubowicz 1994a & 1995a, Splichal 1994).

These determinants highlight the immense scope and challenge of media reform. It is crucial to understand that reforms did not start in a vacuum, but rather had to do away with established structures before a basis for initiatives supporting media independence can be created. These legacies also constitute the basis for current state intervention in the media, which will be elaborated in the following sections.

Media and democracy

The crucial step towards democracy lies in the removal of communist control over all areas of public life. According to Przeworski, "democracy is consolidated when compliance - acting within the institutional framework - constitutes the equilibrium of the decentralized strategies of all relevant political forces" (Przeworski 1991, p. 26). Pointing at the mass media as an important political force, Splichal identifies it as one of the main pillars of civil society, and emphasizes its crucial role as an autonomous mediator between government, business and society (Splichal 1994, p. 10-12). Therefore, democratic consolidation of all relevant political forces, rather than democratic government alone, and the conditions for plurality of information reflecting the diversity of society, become the crucial determinants for the interrelationship between the media and democratic evolution in transition.

Although there are numerous analyses about the correlation between media and democracy, only a few authors have focused on the special context of transition and its relevance for media theory. Downing argues that the influence of the media is not merely restricted to the political arena, but also greatly influences economic, societal and cultural change, and therefore must not be seen in isolation of these factors. (Downing 1996, p. 229). O'Neil criticizes further that «within the current study of democratization in transition systems, dominant analytical approaches tend to focus primarily on particular strategies and resources of elite actors». He finds that the result of such a shortcoming is that «broader state and societal institutions tend to be pushed into the background», and that the media as an important variable for «how the process of transition is sustained, consolidated and institutionalized into a stable democratic system is largely missing from such a perspective» (O'Neil 1996, p. 3).

Jakubowicz provides the most precise framework for analysis, incorporating the interdependence between politics, economics, society and culture by narrowing them down to the most relevant angle for the analysis of this paper. His so-called concept of 'plurality of information' involves (i) *pluriformity*: the existence of different media with different ownership, goals and legal structures, and (ii) *pluralism of content*, involving the media's obligation to reflect and provide facilities for the expression of different points of view, including critical and oppositional ones (Jakubowicz 1995b, p. 80-81). Thus, traditional media theory becomes relevant after the transition of the media has incorporated Jakubowicz' concept of plurality of information. Only then can one argue that the media can assume the role of a 'watchdog' or counter force to politics. In the words of Druout (1995, p. 20) the media has be independent enough to "guarantee pluralism, to oppose the government effectively and to provide 'checks and balances' in the event of shortcomings by traditional political institutions".

Achieving independence

There is of course no general blue print on how to achieve media independence in transition countries. However, there are a few determinants that shape the analysis. Among these are the following:

> *A philosophical debate:* Soon after communism collapsed, two separate schools of thought concerning media policy emerged. Inspired by neo-liberal thinking in the Anglo-American tradition, one school rejects all forms of public regulation and promotes a media policy entirely left up to market forces. Their position is strengthened by international developments of de-regulation and liberalization on the one hand, and the improvement of technology on the other (Jakubowicz 1995a, p. 129). The second school of thought is more concerned with the principle of social justice and equality, and wants to promote equal access to the media as well as some regulation on media contents to ensure quality and balancing of programmes. Stephen Holmes distinguishes between 'free' and 'democratic' communication, introducing the idea that the state can actually be a friend to freedom, yet warning that "partisan control results from the absence, as well as the presence, of state control" (Holmes 1993, p. 41).

> *The general speed and success of political and economic reform in the transition countries*: We can separate three groups of countries in CEE out of which only the first two are relevant for this paper. First, those where transformation into pluralist, free-market democracies is already underway, such as Poland, the Czech Republic, Hungary, Latvia, Slovenia, and Estonia. Second, countries with optimistic prospects for the future, but who are still politically and economically vulnerable, including Slovakia,

Bulgaria, Romania, Lithuania and Croatia. Third, countries whose political and economic future will remain undecided for at least a decade, that is Russia, Ukraine, Belarus, Georgia, Armenia, Azerbeidzhan and Albania (Jakubowicz 1995a, p. 130).

The inevitable steps of media reform that all countries share in common: Jakubowicz identifies the following three stages of reform: *Stage 1* includes dismantling the main features of the old system, de-monopolization and early commercialization of the printed press, the beginning of decentralization and specialization, as well as internationalization. *Stage 2* requires the adoption of a legal framework for press freedom and basic elements of democratization, journalist professionalization and a few successful private media, increasing foreign capital moves, first signs of media concentration, as well as continued trends from stage 1. In *stage 3* the legal framework is further developed to create legal and institutional guarantees of media autonomy and to regulate economic aspects of the media market. Growing political stability will defuse conflicts that prevented processes in the previous stages, increasing - *inter alia* – journalists' professionalism (Jakubowicz 1995a, p. 132).

Throughout the analysis these three stages will remain the underlying focus for the interpretation of media independence. We shall see how philosophical debates translate into politics, in addition to how such clusters echo the economic realities which determine the future progress of media reform. Further, case studies will illustrate the stages of reform.

Economic independence

Independent journalism depends on editorial autonomy, which in turn, is strongly correlated with financial independence. De-monopolizing the printed press and all related media businesses therefore constitutes absolute priority of media reform. Although privatization of the press was one of the first objectives of reform, many governments in CEE managed to maintain economic control of the sector. Most problems occurred in those countries that are classified as being politically and economically vulnerable, as well as those whose future will remain undecided (see previous page).

Generally, privatization of the printed press took place in three waves. At first, political parties obtained existing newspapers, which constituted the first press boom, giving access to dissident movements. Secondly, commercially-oriented domestic publishers began to enter the market, facing tremendous economic problems. Thirdly, foreign investors bought into periodicals, or simply took them over. Initially, there were no provisions governing foreign investment in the press sector (Jakubowicz 1994b, p. 10-11). Obstacles in the development of the printed press were: (i) the impoverishment due to economic reform during the first years, and therefore the (ii) maintenance of Communist distribution and printing facilities, as well as (iii) indirect censorship through new owners. The focus of this section will be on the emerging ownership structures and their influence on the independence of the press.

Euphoria inhibited

As soon as censorship was abolished after the revolutions in 1989, many new newspapers and magazines began to flood the market. In Bulgaria for instance, "the print media became the fastest developing business after the party-state started loosening its grip on power" (Nicholchev 1996, p. 128). The same tendency was observed in all other transition countries, despite the scarcity of printing material, lack of newsprint and problems of distribution. A few figures may illustrate the example: by 1991 it was estimated that 2500 new periodicals had appeared in the Czecho-Slovak market (Giorgi 1995, p. 28). In Slovakia there has been a growth in the number of publications from 326 to 753 between 1989 and 1993 (Skolkay 1996, p. 71). Polish figures reveal that between 1990 an 1992 an average of 100 new titles were issued each month (Giorgi 1995, p. 90). In Bulgaria, a country with barely 8.5 million inhabitants, 928 newspapers and 777 magazines were being published by 1993 (Nicholchev 1996, p. 128-129).

Despite the initial boom of publications, economic realities quickly caught up with the new market and circulation steadily decreased from 1991 onwards. With price liberalization and hyperinflation, the costs of production and cover prices rose rapidly (Mc Nair 1994, p. 122). For example, by 1991 production costs in Czecho-Slovakia had risen 60 per cent in comparison with 1990, the selling price by 27 per cent (Giorgi 1995, p. 28). As economic reforms cut into peoples' living standards, newspapers became more expensive and their purchase an option rather than a commitment. Consequently sales dropped sharply, many papers published only one single issue and went bankrupt thereafter. Advertising as a source of revenue had not yet reached lucrative dimensions, and considering the financial constraints, new solutions for the survival of the publications had to be found. Many of them benefited from the state directly. The main problem was not only that newspapers were poor, but that a lot of politicians would like them to stay poor, or that it is simply 'difficult to be independent when you are poor'.

Economic constraints

Deliberate economic constraints imposed by governments to cripple the print media can take on several forms. Either, they exploit the remaining monopoly on print facilities and distribution, or they chose more subtle methods such as tariffs and taxation to shut out possible private competition. The Ukraine marks an extreme example, in which the government plays its cards through competitive advantage. Subsidies are exchanged against political freedom, which enables 'official' newspapers to sell way below production cost, thereby making it almost impossible for other newspapers to compete. Still holding the monopoly on distribution and print facilities, the Luckashenko government charges private papers almost twice as much per copy distributed, imposes additional import taxes on paper, which inflates paper costs even further. In 1995, subsidized newspapers sold for 4000 coupons, while private publications sold for 15,000 – 30,000 coupons (Chalaby 1998, p. 10-12).

Bulgaria's early days of press freedom were also severely handicapped by the government's monopoly on paper supply, printing and distribution. During the round-table negotiations in 1990, it was even agreed that political party newspapers would be preferably supplied with newsprint. Printing plants were able to set their own prices, change their priority in order of printing, and delay or refuse the production of individual publications. The official press distribution determined the commission percentages, the number of copies for news-stand sale, and the maximum number of subscriptions per publication. Further, publications were not distributed evenly to cities and around the country, rather they often just entered the most convenient news-stand in insufficient quantities.

Even after some larger publishing houses had begun to challenge the state monopoly during the following years, the Bulgarian ministry of finance imposed a heavy value added tax of 18 per cent on all print media activities, including advertising in April 1994. The action was followed by a media strike, which led an official to suggest that "Bulgarians would be better off without the papers" (Nicholchev 1996, p. 132-133). Dailies and weeklies have become a luxury for average Bulgarians. In consequence, many citizens reported in a March 1998 poll that they rely on state-controlled National TV programmes for news. Only 9 percent of the population considered print media as their primary information source. Bulgaria still has no privately owned national television station (Kathimerini, 23 April 1998, p. 3).

Slovakia constitutes a particularly ambiguous case, because examples of deliberate government intervention remain present in the country's every-day news affairs. The state budget in 1995 proposed legal amendments which would have empowered the ministry of culture to designate certain publications as 'non-commercial', thereby subjecting them to a lower rate of taxation. In addition, media outlets with a significant amount of foreign capital were to be taxed three to five times higher than those domestically owned (Skolkay 1996, p. 73). In October 1997, Prime Minister Meciar sought parliamentary support for the introduction of VAT of 23 percent, up from a previous six percent, on domestic newspapers, which display at least 10 percent advertising content.

According to the former Finance Minister, Sergej Kozlik, who resigned in January 1998, the proposal was in line with EU directives[2], and was not expected to impair the periodical press. Only papers that devoted space and financing for their entrepreneurial activities through advertising would be affected (Slovak News Agency 1997a). Yet, advertising revenues are key to the development of the independent press, in particular periodicals. According to the *Syndicate of Slovak Journalists*, the VAT increase would have caused a price increase of 10 crowns a copy, resulting in an average 20 percent drop in circulation, leaving state-owned TV, radio and the government-subsidized press the most likely sources of information for citizens. The only newspaper exempt would have been *Slovenska Republika*, a nationalist daily owned by Meciar's *HDSZ* party (Reuters News Service 1997, The Economist 1997). After strong protests by local and international media, the government proposal was rejected in parliament in December 1997. Alternatively, the government announced to raise revenue by increasing VAT on post and telecom services from six to 23 percent (Slovak News Agency 1997b).

Finding new owners

Achieving plurality of ownership remains an important precondition, not only for the democratization of the press, but also the guarantee of its independence. It is important to note that privatization *per se* neither guarantees plurality of owners, nor editorial autonomy. Therefore, it is important to pay attention to (i) the number of publishing houses and their percentage of market share, (ii) the number of domestic and foreign publishing houses, and (iii) the number of domestic publishing houses with affiliation to political parties or trade unions. Poland, Bulgaria, and Slovakia will serve as examples.

Since Giorgi classified *Polish* media privatization as "one of the most far-reaching and successful privatization projects", the example offers a point of reference for comparisons with less successful cases (Giorgi 1995, p. 80). Poland is also an interesting example because it had one of the most centralized media monopolies under the communist regime. The communist *Workers' Publishing Cooperative* (referred to as RSW), was privatized in March 1990. It included publishing and printing houses, photo agencies, newspaper kiosks, press clubs and two media research institutes. In addition, a law on the Liquidation of the RSW was passed, as was a *Liquidation Committee*, appointed by the Prime Minister, which monitored the privatization process. It was further agreed that priority would be given to employee cooperatives.

By 1993, the *Liquidation Committee* declared the termination of its proceedings (Giorgi 1995, p. 75-79).

During the first phase of the liquidation, *Solidarity* turned out to be the big winner, acquiring three influential regional dailies in Gdansk and Bialystock, and a large number of shares in eight additional newspapers. Many political parties fought over the purchase of well-known titles, most notably was Walesa's support to sell *Express Wieczorny,* a popular Warsaw afternoon daily to the *Center Alliance.* The *Social Democratic Party* bought a number of former communist papers, other titles were purchased by the *National Christian Association*, the *Independent Poland Confederation*, who enjoyed the support of the Catholic Church, and the *Democratic Union* (Giorgi 1995, p. 77-78).

In many instances, the political opposition protested against the allowances made for journalists' cooperatives, fearing the acquisition of a large market by the former nomenclatura. Journalists' cooperatives took a particularly strong stand in the local press, which was dependent on the funding of firms or credit institutions owned by the former nomenclatura. Pressure from trade unions to safeguard jobs of media professionals contributed to their persistence (Downing 1996, p. 148). Despite all criticism, Giorgi notes that by 1993, the Polish press was dominated by private and cooperative owners, signaling the onset of plurality (Giorgi 1995, p. 80).

In terms of foreign ownership, the *Liquidation Committee* initially took a cautious approach. The goal was to "regulate the privatization process with respect to both domestic and foreign investors in order to ensure a balanced representation of actors in the media" (Giorgi 1995, p. 20). However, economic pressures left no alternative. Foreign investors were finally welcomed to fill the financial gap. In 1996, the largest foreign investors in the Polish print media were *Cox Enterprises* (USA), *Robert Hersant* (France), *Orka ASA* (Norway), *Neue Passauer Presse* (Germany), *Jorg Marquard* (Switzerland) and *Nicola Grauso* (Italy). They owned 56 percent of the total share of Polish national dailies (Goban-Klas 1996, p. 27). In order to limit the extent of foreign media concentration, the Polish government is currently preparing additional regulation, thus implementing Jakubowicz' final stage of media reform.

The *Bulgarian* print media took a very different route towards independence. Contrary to the Polish pre-1989 experience, there was no underground press. The official press was further tightened during the years of *glasnost* and *perestroika* as a deliberate attempt of the *Communist Party* leader, Theodor Zhivkov, to distance himself from Gorbachev. Even after Zhivkov lost power in 1989, journalists of the official press played a key role in the development of the media. The first wave of new publications was therefore directly connected to political parties. The *Bulgarian Socialist Democratic Party* published the daily *Svoboden Narod*, the opposition *Union of Democratic Forces* launched *Demokratsia*, and the *former Communist Party* published the daily *Rabotnichesko Delo* under the new name *Duma*. For a long time, *Duma's* and *Demokratsia's* editorial lines reflected merely party-political confrontations (Nicholchev 1996, p. 124-130).

Although a second wave of new and private entries into the newspaper market followed within one year, *Duma*, as well as another formerly Communist paper, *Trud* (Labor), have managed to remain market leaders. Bulgarian researchers explain that the relatively "rapid privatization of the print media could be seen as a pre-emptive defense against retributive legislation punishing old-regime organizations" (Nicholchev 1996, p. 130). In addition, the lack of bankruptcy laws enabled many small publishers to survive despite rising production costs, kept alive by financial institutions that indirectly supported politicians or political parties (Kolarova & Dimitrov 1993, p. 49). *Radio Free Europe* reported that newspapers backed by an influential financial group, party or trade union had the best chance of survival. But newspapers with solid financial backing often had to pay for that support with editorial restrictions (Krause 1995, p. 46). Whereas the direct influence of parties and unions was much stronger during the first five years of transition, financial influence became a more subtle tool of intervention thereafter.

For a long time the tabloid *24 Chasa* was the market leader, which belonged to the *168 Press Group*. Its main rival was *Trud*, controlled by *Media Holding*. Both papers had readership shares two to three times higher than their competitors. *168 Press Group* however, experienced a sudden fall from its leading position in 1994. The company was controlled by the *Mollov* investment group, which belonged to a newly founded *First Private Bank*. The bank allegedly absorbed many ex-communist funds, and began to accredit selected companies, such as *168*. In order to buy its own printing press, the company indebted itself, and repaid its gratitude with a faithful editorial line in favor of then Prime Minister Zhan Videnov, formerly a Communist Party *cadre* under Zhivkov. The bank collapsed when rumors about investments caused panic and customers claimed their money back, in its wake also rendering the *168 Press Group* bankrupt. *24 Chasa* was not only famous for its financial scam with the government, but also for its parodies on the other papers' confrontations between ex-Communists and Liberal owners. Today, confrontations between parties through newspapers has more or less stopped, since they have lost large parts of their readership. Ironically, new foreign owners such as the German media conglomerate *WAZ* entered the Bulgarian market in 1995, absorbing two conglomerates with one stone: they bought all shares of *24 Chasa*, while also acquiring shares of its political opponent *Trud*.

Although *Slovakia* is considered one of the more successful transition countries in terms of economic reform, its shortfalls in the process of democratization have been widely condemned by western institutions. Fisher (1997, p. 13) argues that the country is "heading toward international isolation". Slovakia's recent example of direct censorship through indirect ownership in the printed press illustrates the twisted ways in which Meciar's government merges political and economic influence. The following case study of Tatiana Repkova, the former editor in chief of *Narodna Obroda*, a business daily, illustrates a telling story. Slovakia's newspaper market consists of a few leading papers. *Novy Cas*, is the main tabloid, covering 27 percent of the country's readership. The two-leftist dailies, *Pravda* and *Praca,* follow with 13 and 8 percent respectively, compared to 6 and 4 percent readership for the right-of-center dailies *Sme* and *Narodna Obroda*. In 1995, *Narodna Obroda* and *Novy Cas* were the only major papers with significant foreign ownership, the former majority-owned by the French media magnate Robert Hersant, the latter by an Austrian company. *Sme* and *Pravda* came under the control of *Harvard Investment*, which is connected to Vladimir Lexa, a former top-ranking communist and father of Meciar's close ally Ivan Lexa (Fisher 1995).

Narodna Obroda started in 1990 as a joint-stock company owned by journalists. However, due to management and financial problems (Fisher 1997), 49 percent of its shares were sold to Robert Hersant in 1992, who then sold his shares to a German printer, retaining the company name NOFRA (*Narodna Obroda France*). NOFRA kept running into financial problems and the journalists sold the remaining 51 percent interest to *Topmedia*, a subsidiary of a Bratislava advert agency. By the time Tatiana Repkova took charge as editor in chief in January 1996, rumors were spreading that the largest Slovak steel mill, *VSZ Kosice*, with close ties to the Meciar government, was behind *Topmedia*. Alexander Rezes, former vice-president of VSZ, became minister of transportation and telecommunications in 1996. Finally, in March 1996, all shares were sold to VSZ, followed by the complete buy-out two month later when the company also acquired all German shares (Repkova 1997, p. 86-88).

The lessons we can learn from these examples shed light on many new emerging problems in the newspaper market in CEE. Most important, the story of *Narodna Obroda*, along with the Bulgarian example of *24 Chasa*, illustrate that private owners do not guarantee independence. Because capitalism in CEE is emerging without capital, many domestic companies entering the print market are those that base their wealth on ex-Communist networks. Foreign ownership seems to represent no guarantee for a safe way out of government interference. However, new private owners may create their own monopolies, such as the WAZ group in Bulgaria, *Robert Hersant*, or *Neue Passauer Presse* in other countries. Their interference can take two forms: WAZ for instance, avoids trouble with the government because it seeks to acquire more shares in the privatization of telecommunications and broadcasting sectors. The so-called 'advertising propaganda', or business 'advertorial', illustrating the dictatorship of business interests, is another case in point. Requests by *nouveau-riche* industrial owners, are based on a barter-scheme: "We let you get rich, you repay it by space and attention in your newspaper". Such examples also highlight another dilemma of journalists in Eastern Europe. Their salaries are often so low, that young talented people prefer careers elsewhere. For others, the sheer fear of redundancy often results in self-censorship. It often proves safer and more profitable not to investigate a story, or withhold information, than risk to get fired.

Political independence

While the printed press is more or less successfully struggling for its independence, television and broadcasting are still under tight control by all governments in CEE. So-called 'media wars' regarding the reluctance of the political elite to de-regulate audiovisual media are one of the greatest democratic challenges for post-communist governments. The confrontations reflected the struggle of competencies between different branches of the government over the appointment of regulatory and management positions of the audio-visual institutions, as well as the constitutional legacies of Communist media legislation. Related controversies include the delay of new media laws, the allocation of air time on TV and radio during election campaigns, the provision of licenses for new private stations, questions of budgetary control, and limitations of foreign ownership. Disputes over instances of defamation and libel constitute a legal debate that concern print and the audio-visual media alike.

For many reasons the audio-visual sector has always been regarded as more sensitive to state intervention in CEE. First, TV and broadcasting were the main tool of communist propaganda. Therefore, the density of households with television sets is very high. Second, TV's impact was accentuated by the economic vulnerability of the newspaper market, causing rising prices and poor distribution. Third, there is an international trend favoring televised news broadcasting, rendering image and personality of political figures ever more important (Downing 1996, p. 174). According to the Hungarian analyst Hankiss, "the TV screen is [..] the only window for people on public life, the only means of participation in politics, the only real source of beliefs and identities" (Hankiss 1994, p. 307).

The media wars

Hungary marks a special case in the struggle for de-regulation of audiovisual media. Whereas most other CEE countries adopted new media laws and created new regulatory bodies for television and broadcasting within the first two years of transition, the Hungarian media law was only passed in December 1995. In the early 1990s, the conservative Prime Minister Josef Antall spoke in favor of maintaining the media as a public service, whereas the opposition sought a fully independent media, with all six parliamentary parties choosing the directors (Szilagyi 1996). In this respect, Hankiss notes that Hungary's opposition at the time of the revolution was already comparatively pluralistic, which made it difficult for the government to agree on issues of reform, particularly in the early stages (Hankiss 1994, p. 295).

The 'media war' began in 1991, when the Antall government maintained to be threatened by biased reporting of the printed press, and subsequently turned its attention to television and broadcasting. The chairmen of television and broadcasting were two independent political scientists, Elemer Hankiss and Csaba Gombar, who attempted to transform the party-controlled institutions into European-type media companies. Hoping to rally popular support, right-wing groups and the governing parties alike accused the chairmen of both institutions of jeopardizing national Hungarian values by commercializing and Americanizing national television. Asking for a "better balance", they also rejected any kind of criticism directed against state officials (Hankiss 1994, p. 301).

In June 1992, the struggles for influence between the Prime Minister and the President began. Prime Minister Antall proposed that President Goncz should dismiss Hankiss and Gombar. Lacking a new media law that would have entitled him to such an action, he invoked a 1974 decree which gave the government such powers. Goncz, trying to assert his presidential authority in the absence of new legislation, refused to sign the dismissal, claiming the responsibility to guarantee press freedom. The Constitutional Court resolved the issue, ruling the 1974 decree unconstitutional. However, it validated its application until a new law was passed. When Hankiss and Gombar finally did file their resignation to the President in 1993, a new controversy between Antall and Goncz began, because Antall tried to surpass Goncz by accepting the resignation. Goncz protested, claiming that only he had the exclusive right to accept or dismiss the request (Hankiss 1994, p. 304). He finally refused. It remained unclear to whom Hankiss and Gombar were ultimately accountable. Gabor Nahlik and Laszlo Csus, both pro-Antall representatives, took over the posts of television and radio chairmen. As the 1994 elections approached, 129 radio employees were dismissed by Csus. Numerous strikes followed. As it turned out, the interference of the governing *Hungarian Democratic Forum* into the media played a crucial role in their subsequent defeat at the polls.

The new legislation, which was passed in December 1995, constitutes a serious attempt to disengage politics form the media. It provides for the creation of three public foundations, one for Hungarian Television, one for radio and one for *Duna TV*. They will be overseen by the *National Radio and Television Board* (ORTT), whose eight members are elected by parliament. ORTT will also manage the frequency distribution. The new law requires the privatization of two of the three terrestrial television frequencies, as well as one statewide radio station. Although the new law is the result of a compromise, it has been criticized for many reasons. Halami states that party politics have now become 'institutionalized' through the appointment procedure of the ORTT. Its members are elected by the different parliamentary parties and the president is appointed by the head of state and the head of government. Together, they establish a so-called complaints committee which then decides on the balance of content (Halami 1997, p. 68, IPI World Press Freedom Review 1997).

The *Polish* media wars took a different angle. Poland's opposition was united in the *Solidarnosc* movement and was therefore able to push its demands more comprehensively. During the 1989 *Round Table Talks* a three-step plan was agreed for the de-regulation of state control, and a law on television and broadcasting was eventually passed in 1992 (Sparks & Reading 1994, p. 255). The 'media war' started in 1994 over the allocation of airwaves. The second controversial issue is the debate about ethics in journalism, similar to the debate on national values in Hungary. Before the battle over the airwaves began, a moratorium on broadcasting frequencies, adopted by the *Sejm* in 1991, determined the rules of the game. The 1992 law included a clause which obliges public as well as private journalists to "accept Christianity as the basic ethical value" (Goban-Klas 1996, p. 30). In addition, the law stipulated the creation of the *National Broadcasting Council* (KRRT), which consists of 9 members, nominated by the Senate, the *Sejm* and the President of the Republic. The Council's powers include the supervision of programming, the assignment of frequencies and licenses to broadcast and the allocation of income from license fees (Downing 1996, p. 149). Because of its obsession as the guardian of Christian values it was jokingly referred to as the 'National Broadcasting *Inquisition*' (Goban-Klas 1996, p. 30, emphasis added). The law also transformed *Polish Television* (TVP) from a state enterprise into a shareholder company, with one single shareholder, namely the Treasury Department. Hence the finance minister not only gained indirect influence over programming, but also the right to nominate one member of TVP's supervisory board (Kaprinski 1996). In a word, party politics seem perfectly institutionalized.

In 1994, then President Walesa launched a series of appointments and dismissals in the KRRT. In January 1995, the KRRT issued a broadcasting license to *PolSat*, the only commercial channel at the time. Without offering any proof, Walesa suggested that Rupert Murdoch's *News Corporation* would use the channel to enter Polish broadcasting. When the Council dismissed his complaint, he dismissed its president, Marek Markiewicz. The *Supreme Administrative Court* ruled that the allocation of the license for *PolSat* was perfectly valid. Walesa proceeded to replace the Council's chairman with Marek Jurek form the *Christian National Union*, hoping to gain the party's support for the November 1995 presidential elections. In June 1995, the *Sejm* voted by a large majority in favor of an amendment that would deprive the president of his right to nominate the chairman of the KRRT (Downing 1996, p. 149-150, Kaprinski 1996). Further incidences of government intervention after the former Communists returned to power in 1993 were the dismissal of Maciej Pawlicki, head of the popular channel TVP1. He was accused of airing 'improper' programs critical of the communist past. Before the general elections in September 1997, the KRRT appointed a new supervisory board for public television and radio companies. "In each case, most of the nine new members have close ties to the *Democratic Left Alliance* or the *Peasant's Party*" (The

Economist 1997). The Economist concludes that apparently, "old habits die hard" and "this is not the sort of behavior expected from a prospective member of the European Union" (ibid).

Both countries illustrate tendencies common across CEE. First, in those countries that did not draft entirely new constitutions after 1989, updating media legislation was considerably delayed. However, it is only too obvious that the legal vacuum was a welcome tool for the ruling parties to secure their position in the media until they were willing to compromise on a new law (Sparks & Reading 1994, p. 259). Second, the new institutional framework which was to provide for the democratization of media organizations, strongly reflects party politics at the time, since compromise was always born out of a barter between government and opposition. Thirdly, the influence of strong personalities, such as Antall or Walesa, is paramount. Finally, one must also be careful not to reach the conclusion that the media wars were solely instigated by former Communists, trying to cling on to power. By contrast, it was the first dissident government in Hungary that fought the media war, playing similar cards against protagonists they were once opposing.

Beware of libel

Granting freedom of speech alone is not enough. Governments in CEE have found a new form of censorship: *libel laws*. Ambiguous 'ethical' considerations were transformed into law, making libel cases one of the most frequent law suits in the region. The legal amendments concern (i) the *Civil Code*, which protects the dignity and reputation of citizens, and (ii) the *Penal Code*, which includes penalties for insulting officials, slander, incitement, etc. Defamation and libel are well disputed legal issues in the West. Taking the example of the US, after fifty years of conflict, the Supreme Court has "subsumed hate-speech and group defamation within its more general assumption that most forms of content based restrictions of speech are unconstitutional" (Stone 1994, p. 82). The underlying rationale is that governments cannot be trusted to make judgments about which ideas can and cannot be legitimately aired in public debate.

Compared to the US, Central and East European constitutions attempt to incorporate the rather controversial dilemma that unrestrained speech might endanger social stability. The ambiguity lies in the identification of factors that might do so. The most contested code is therefore the Penal Code, which determines what qualifies as offensive against the interests of the country. In *Hungary*, "whoever uses an expression that is offensive or demeaning to the Hungarian nation, any nationality, people, faith, or race shall be punished by imprisonment of up to one year or a fine" (Sajo 1994, p. 83). The *Polish* Penal Code turns against statements, (i) "that publicly insult, ridicule, and deride the Polish Republic, its political system, or its principal organs punishable between 6 months and 8 years of imprisonment", and (ii) that "offending religious sentiment through public speech is punishable by a fine or a 2-year prison term" (Post-Soviet Media Law & Policy Newsletter 1997). *Slovakia's* recently passed 'anti-subversion' law allows up to 3-year prison sentences for anyone who knowingly spreads false information about the republic. Also, the law provides jail sentences for "anyone organizing public rallies aimed at harming the constitutional system, Slovakia's territorial integrity, defense ability or independence". The law has been widely condemned in the West, making it the most-watched media development of the IPI in 1996.[3]

Respecting the 'dignity' of individuals is a completely different matter, rendering the defamation of politicians a particularly delicate affair. The most important issue is the attitude of politicians toward journalists. An illustrative comment stems from Poland's current president of public TV, Rysard Mlazek. According to him,

> the claim that a journalist is a representative of society defies the distribution of roles in a democratic state. A journalist must follow the guidelines set by his superiors. [..] Society is the state and its democratic structures, and television should offer its services to them. It should not aspire at expressing independent opinions, because such opinions are formulated by parliament and other representatives of the state (Post-Soviet Media Law & Policy Newsletter 1996).

The former Czech Prime Minister Vaclav Klaus was well-known for his rather infamous remark that "journalists are the biggest enemies of mankind" (Kettle 1995). In Hungary, a journalist was sued for quoting an accusation by one politician against another, even though it was made at a press conference. In other countries, such as Slovakia, Bulgaria, Romania and the CIS, measures against defamation include harassment, persecution, even kidnapping (IPI World Press Freedom Review 1997). To avoid trouble, the Slovak Prime Minister Meciar suggested that "journalists should practice ethical self-regulation" (Skolkay 1996, p. 75). Defamation and libel laws in CEE are ambiguous because they can be used to blackmail papers or indirectly result in self-censorship. The laws are often phrased in a manner where it is 'easy to put in jail any journalist who does not fit the government'. The fear of libel seriously damages the freedom of speech in CEE. The number of criminal and civil libel suits against journalists in CEE is a matter of concern. They continue to be used by public officials and businessmen as an instrument of harassment against investigative reporters and editors.

Future Perspectives

Many governments are currently focusing on introducing new legislation to limit foreign capital involvement in both the print and broadcasting media. Jakubowicz warns that due to the limits of domestic capital, many small local media companies will not be able to survive in a highly competitive market with foreign owners (Jakubowicz 1994b, p. 43-45). Especially, the emergence of private foreign monopolies, such as the American-owned *Central European Media Enterprises Corp.*(CME) set an alarming sign for the need of further regulation. CME now controls stations in seven CEE countries, reaching 95 million viewers. The company is about to explore markets in the Balkans, Baltics and the CIS (ICFJ 1997). Splichal identifies two types of public service broadcasting. They range from the British model of *centrally controlled* market economy, as is illustrated by the BBC, to the *regulated* market economy, prominently practiced in Sweden and Austria. These types represent different options for the control of (i) subsidies, (ii) the competition between private and public channels, and (iii) the allocation of air time as well as use of publicly owned production facilities. Although the discussions about the nature of broadcasting regulation have been neglected in CEE, Splichal assumes that traditional contents regulation, infrastructure policies to ensure universal access, regulation of common standards, and free public services shape broadcasting regulations in post-communist countries (Splichal 1994, p. 140-143).

There are numerous debates whether the downfall of the Communist regimes in 1989 was a revolution or merely a regime change. Certainly, there was no revolution in the Central and East European media. However, developments in the media also illustrate a good example for the general perception about the persistence of state influence over many sectors of society. The legacy of 'old-think' is an important contributor to the newly emerging media systems in CEE. This is not to say that no progress has been achieved in the media. By contrast, quoting Hankiss, "it is better to have a war of words and political strategies around the media than to have a war fought with tanks and guns in the fields" (Hankiss 1994, p. 293). The 'media wars' have illustrated the importance of the rule of law, the conduct of conflict without using violence, and the fact that citizens' initiatives can challenge politicians. This, however, may be cold comfort to those countries who are still at the beginning of the struggle for media independence.

According to Przeworski, democracy is about uncertainty, about parties loosing elections and the uncontrollability of outcomes. It is a "devolution of power from people to a set of rules" (Przeworski 1991, p. 10-14). The struggles for media independence suffered from the dilemma that those men who were to disengage from public life were also those making the rules, trying to guarantee the controllability of outcomes in their own interest. Although the media will remain politically sensitive, it will only be able to assert its independence in legal, institutional and economic terms at the point in time when governments have settled on a defined set of rules, and amendments are no longer made out of clientelistic motives.

Looking ahead, the print and audio-visual media have one important asset guaranteeing future independence form every-day politics: the influx of foreign investors, who bring resources, personnel and diversity. The new task for the governments in CEE is therefore to provide adequate regulation. The printed press needs more defined laws on ownership concentration, in order to avoid the creation of new monopolies. Television and radio are also becoming increasingly interesting for investors who hope to benefit from new advertising markets and telecoms' privatization. Regulation needs to be passed on the limitation of foreign participation in franchises and joint ventures. Considering the tremendous license fees paid by commercial stations to get access to airwaves, the media is a lucrative business, for private and public owners alike. Thus, the process towards greater press freedom is irreversible because governments find themselves under domestic and international pressure. Most important, media independence is increasingly recognized as a fundamental determinant of democratic development and respect for human rights. Since most transition countries seek integration into international political and economic organizations, most notably the European Union, these pressures work in favor of governments' withdrawal from media intervention. Yet, establishing media freedom will remain an ongoing process, which needs to be re-affirmed in daily practice.

Notes

1   Primary material was retrieved through personal correspondence with Tatiana Repkova, the former editor of the Slovak business daily *Narodna Obroda*, Veneta Jenkova, the Bulgaria correspondent for the Austrian daily *Die Presse*, as well as an interview with the managing editor Adam Feinstein of the *IPI World Press Freedom Review*, a publication of the *International Press Institute* in London. Additional background information was provided by material from the media conference *Europe Media Forum: Traditions & Transitions*, held by the *Freedom Forum* in London in May 1997. I am grateful to the editor, Dr Jens Bastian, for investigative comments on the contribution.
2   The EU Council Directive (77/388/EEC), which has been in effect as a recommendation for EU associate-member countries

(including Slovakia), regulates VAT rates for goods and services, including the periodical press. According to this Directive, reduced VAT rates can be applied only for such periodicals that do not focus on display or classified advertising, or have erotic or pornographic content.

3   According to the IPI, the amendment was passed as a deal between Meciar and coalition members of the ultra-right Slovak National Party. The law on the Protection of the Republic was in exchange for its support for the ratification of the Slovak-Hungarian Bilateral Treaty.

References

Business Eastern Europe (1996), 'Glued to the Box', October 7th, 1996.

Chalaby, J-K. (1996), 'The Public Sphere and the Media in Eastern Europe: the Case of Ukraine', *LSE-European Institute Publication*: London.

Comparative Analysis of Independent Media Development in Post-Communist Russia and Ukraine, on, *http://www.internews.org*.

Connors, S. et al. (1995), 'Differing Views on Government Control', *Transition*, October 6th, 1995.

Denton, N. (1993), 'Hungary Builds Capitalism Without Capital', *Financial Times*, November 1st, 1993.

Downing, J. (1996), *Internationalizing Media Theory: Transition, Power, Culture*, Sage Publications: London.

Druout, G. (1995), 'Mass Media and Political Power in a Pluralist Democracy', *Implementation of Constitutional Provisions Regarding Mass Media in a Pluralist Democracy*, Council of Europe Publishing.

The Economist (1997), 'Televisual Coup', August 16th, 1997.

Europe Media Forum (1997), *Traditions & Transitions*, Freedom Forum, Conference Report, May 29-30 (1997), London.

European Media Institute, 'Media in the CIS', on, *http://www.internews.org*.

Fisher, S. (1995), 'Slovak Media Under Pressure', *Transition*, October 6th, 1995.

----, (1997), 'Slovakia Heads Toward International Isolation', *Transition*, February 7th, 1997.

Giorgi, L. (1995), *The Post-Socialist Media: What Power the West?*, Avebury: Aldershot.

Goban-Klas, T. (1996), 'Politics Versus the Media in Poland: A Game Without Rules', *Journal of Communist Studies*, Vol. 12, No 4, pp. 24-41.

Hague, R. (1992/ed), *Comparative Government and Politics*, Macmillan, London.

Halami, G. (1997), 'Ungarn: Medien und Recht', *Transit*, Vol. 13, pp. 66-71.

Hankiss, E. (1994), 'The Hungarian Media War of Independence: A Stevenson Lecture, 1992', *Media, Culture and Society*, Vol. 16, pp. 293-312.

Havel, V. (1995), 'A Soul of a Soul', *Media Studies*, Summer, pp. 25.

Holmes, S. (1993), 'Media Freedoms in Eastern Europe', *East European Constitutional Review*, Vol. 2, No 3, pp. 41-42.

Hopkinson, N. (1996) 'Strengthening the Media in the Developing World and Eastern Europe', *Wilton Park Paper*, No 115, pp. 1-29.

ICFJ (1997), *Clearinghouse on the Central and East European Press*, No 27, May 1997.

Jakubowicz, K. (1994), 'Equality for Downtrodden, Freedom for Free: Changing Perspectives on Social Communication in Central and Eastern Europe', *Media, Culture and Society*, Vol. 16, pp. 271-292.

----, (1994b), 'Study on Media Concentration and Pluralism in Central and East European Countries', Secretariat Memorandum Prepared by the *Directorate of Human Rights*, Council of Europe.

----, (1995a), 'Media Within and Without the State: Press Freedom in Eastern Europe', *Journal of Communication*, Vol. 45, No 4 , pp. 125-139.

----, (1995b), 'Legislative Guarantees of Plurality of Information sources', *Implementation of Constitutional Provisions Regarding Mass Media in a Pluralist Democracy*, Council of Europe Publishing.

Kaprinski, J. (1996), 'Politicians Endanger Independence of Polish Public TV', *Transition*, April 19th, 1996.

Kathimerini, 23 April 1998, *Bulgaria 1997: Skin-deep Reform*, p. 3.

Keane, J. (1991), *The Media and Democracy*, Polity Press, London.

Kettle, S. (1995), 'The Czech Republic Struggles to Define an Independent Press', *Transition*, October 6th, 1995.

Kolarova, R. and Dimitrov, D. (1993), 'Media Wars in Sofia', *East European Constitutional Review*, Vol. 2, No 3, pp. 48-49.

Krause, S. (1995), 'Purges and Progress in Bulgaria', *Transition*, October 6th, 1995.

Lanczi, A. and O'Neil, P. (1996), 'Pluralization and Politics of Media Change in Hungary', *Journal of Communist Studies*, Vol. 12, No 4, pp. 83-99.

Lis, J. (1995), 'State the Obvious', *Business Eastern Europe*, August 7th, 1995.

McNair, B. (1994), 'Media in Post-Soviet Russia: An Overview', *European Journal of Communication*, Vol. 9, pp. 115-135.

Milton, A. K. (1996), 'News Media Reform in Eastern Europe: A Cross-National Comparison', *Journal of Communist Studies*, Vol. 12, No 4, pp. 6-21.

Nicholchev, I. (1996), 'Polarization and Diversification in the Bulgarian Press', *Journal of Communist Studies*, Vol. 12, No 4, pp. 125-145.

OMRI Daily Digest, on, *http:/www omri.cz*.

O'Neil, P. (1996), 'Introducing Media Reform and Democratization in Eastern Europe', *Journal of Communist Studies*, Vol. 12, No 4, pp. 1-6.

Post-Soviet Media Law & Policy Newsletter (1993-1997), on, *http://www.ctr.columbia.edu*.

Post-Soviet Media Law & Policy Newsletter, 'Zycie Warsawy', April 15, 1996, on, *http://www.ctr.columbia.edu*.

Przeworski, A. (1991), *Democracy and the Market: Political and Economic Reforms in Eastern Europe and Latin America*, Cambridge University Press: Cambridge, UK.

Radio Free Europe/Radio Liberty, *Human Rights Report*, on, *http://www.rferl.org*.

Repkova, T. (1997), 'Steely Grip on a Slovak Daily', *Transitions*, June, pp. 86-89.

Reuters, November 11th, 1997.

Rutland, P. (1996), 'What Are They Watching?', *Transition*, April 19th, 1996.

Sajo, A. (1994), 'Hate Speech for Hostile Hungarians', *East European Constitutional Review*, Vol. 3, No 2, pp. 82-87.

Skolkay, A. (1996), 'Journalists, Political Elites and the Post-Communist Public: The Case of Slovakia', *Journal of Communist Studies*, Vol. 12, No 4, pp. 61-81.

Slovak News Agency, October 31st, 1997.

----, December 12th, 1997.

Sparks, C. and Reading, A. (1994), 'Understanding Media Change in East Central Europe', *Media, Culture and Society*, Vol. 16, pp. 243-270.

Splichal, S. (1994), *Media Beyond Socialism*, Westview Press: Boulder, Colorado.

Stone, G. (1994), 'Hate Speech and the US Constitution', *East European Constitutional Review*, Vol. 3, No 2, pp. 78-82.

Szilagyi, Z. (1996), 'Hungary has a Broadcast Media Law, At Last', *Transition*, April 19th, 1996.

World Press Freedom Review (1996/97), *IPI Report*, December 1996/January 97.

6 Print media in Romania: Struggling for independence and democratic change

Gudrun Lingner

Introduction

Under the dictatorship of Nicolae Ceausescu a particular type of Communism developed in Romania, which also found its reflection in the press. Until the collapse of the system in 1989/90, few other Eastern European states had twisted the truth to such an extent, and the art of misinformation was skillfully practiced. Even if state television presented Ceausescu, the 'genius of the Carpathian Mountains', in front of huge, ready-to-harvest corn fields, this was far from implying that these fields actually existed.

Distortions of the truth for decades have left deep scars in Romanian society. The habit of reporting fictitious events and remaining silent about reality has discredited the press in the eyes of most Romanian people. It has also created a generation of journalists who hardly seemed suited to constitute the 'fourth power' of the new democracy. During the December 1989 revolution the conditions for the creation of an independent press were bad: anything beyond the intimate family circle provoked mistrust, while corruption and inertia, being necessary for survival, had long become a way of life. Sadly, it is precisely these same characteristics which today are proving to be entrenched legacies for the consolidation of democratic structures in Romania.

In order to set up a stable democracy, it is not enough to introduce reforms on an economic level, i.e. creating new institutions. A durable political transformation can only be guaranteed through social changes and the creation of an attentive public opinion (Merkel 1994, p. 3). Democracy in Romania can only be consolidated if each citizen develops his or her individual power of initiative and responsibility. It is necessary to create a civil society as a solid foundation. This certainly holds true for all democracies, but in particular for those in the former Communist countries. In the Eastern European states undergoing transformation official censorship no longer exists and a large number of new media has been created. Everywhere journalists are setting up trade unions in order to defend their rights. Irreversible steps have been taken. However, the media in most of the former Communist countries are far from enjoying real independence. A study carried out by Freedom House in 1995 found that only five former Communist countries possess a free press (Connors et al. 1995, p. 3). Most governments are still applying direct or indirect pressure on the media. At the same time, due to technical developments (internet, satellite and digital television) it is becoming more and more difficult for authoritarian regimes to control the flow of information in their countries. The new micro-electronic technologies enable citizens to communicate in previously unthinkable ways.

Throughout Eastern Europe journalists are struggling under difficult economic conditions for the freedom of expression which theoretically already exists. Usual Western professional standards of reporting are often not respected, sometimes unconsciously, sometimes in the name of so-called 'cultural characteristics'. As a result of pronounced political conviction, many publications have lost their credibility. The construction of public opinion and civil society remains difficult. This should not, however, lead us to carelessly abandon the media and journalists of former Communist countries to their fate. The condition of a whole society is mirrored in the situation of its media and the press can create a public opinion, which may garner enough power to shape the system. It allows for pluralistic representation of interests and the construction of a social consensus (Sparks 1992). A reasonable, informed public opinion plays a central mediating role between citizens and their state institutions.

In March 1996, Aaron Rhodes, executive director of the *International Helsinki Federation for Human Rights*, expressed in Bucharest an ironic opinion on the inflationist use of the slogan *civil society*: "In fact, after 'coke' and 'ok', these are probably some of the most well known words in the region. At the same time, they mean different things to different people" (Rhodes 1996, p. 143). The following contribution is situated in this assessment.[1] Assuming that the press plays a central part in the effort to anchor a new beginning in society, the study analyses the situation of Romanian print media willing to support democratic development.

In 1996 the author spent several months working as a journalist for two representative Romanian newspapers in Bucharest, *Adevarul* and *România Libera*. At the time of writing (April 1998), *Adevarul* is the daily newspaper with the greatest print run. It originates from *Scîntea*, the former publication of the RCP. *Adevarul* had been close to Iliescu's government in 1990/1991, gaining more independence in the following years. The second great national daily newspaper in Romania is *România Libera,* which sympathizes with the political parties of the *Democratic Convention*, who won the presidential and parliamentary elections in November 1996. Eight years after the Romanian revolution, *România Libera* had become a major forum for the political opposition to the then Iliescu-government.

The author's objective was to inquire if the two Romanian newspapers with the highest print runs can be considered as "a pillar of democracy" (Keane 1992). This first hand experience forms the basis for the case studies and the recommendations addressed in the conclusions. In order to understand the development of Romanian print media, and analyze the nature of their contemporary role, it seemed useful to anchor this contribution on field research. In fact, most of the information about Romanian print media was not available outside the country. However, in an international comparison with other Balkan states, Romania takes first place with a daily sale of 322 newspapers per thousand people (Stamenov 1993, p. 4).

Civil society, press and democratization in Romania

Since the Romanian revolution in 1989 many statements have been made about the so-called "Romanian exception", the "Romanian paradox", or the "Romanian authoritarianism". Samuel Huntington for example, analyzing the opportunities for democratic consolidation in various parts of the world, concluded: "Finally, Sudan and Romania seemed especially deficient in the conditions that might support the maintenance of democracy" (Huntington 1991, p. 278). As major causes for this Romanian "inability", Huntington identified the indifferent external environment, the lack of democratic experience after World War II, and the violence involved in the December 1989 events (ibid. p. 270-280).

Following this argument, many studies about Romania predicted a shift towards authoritarianism. The "Western culture thesis", developed by George F. Kennan, saw Romanians divided into two scenarios: either (i) Transylvania being the "boundary of Western Christendom in 1500", (ii) or to face a new authoritarian regime. According to Huntington's controversial idea about the "clash of civilizations" (ibid. 1993), the Eastern part of Romania belonged to "Orthodox Christianity" which, together with Islam, represents an antagonistic counterpart to "Western Europe". When Ion Iliescu and the PDSR won the presidential and parliamentary elections in 1992, these assumptions appeared to be confirmed for such critical Balkan observers.

Alina Mungiu, a young Romanian scientist, called her study on the Romanian mentality after 1989 "the story of misunderstandings". She maintained that the idea of an ingenious "Romanian authoritarianism" has to be contested. "When communism was enthroned in post-war Romania there were no pre-requisites for a totalitarian regime in Romanian society" (Mungiu 1995, p. 320). As a consequence, there is no need to blame the "Romanian exception". If people learned to be passive and docile then, they can learn to adopt democratic values now. Mihai Coman, who analyzed the impact of the press during the 1992 campaign considered that if the press had changed after the revolution, it had not necessarily been a positive development: "In the 1992 election campaign the press contributed to an atmosphere of confusion, rumor mongering, partisanship, and emotionalism. Its efficacy as a tool of re-education, re-socialization, and information is at best highly questionable and most likely non-existent" (Coman and Gross 1994, p. 237).

Nevertheless, some things have changed in Romania. In November 1996, the former Communists lost both presidential and parliamentary elections, and the independent press largely contributed to the success of the *Democratic Convention* (Gabanyi 1996, p. 796). Without freedom of the press and their criticism of the post-Ceausescu rulers, the political volte-face and new beginning in November 1996 would not have been possible. Although a general lack of professionalism still persists in the Romanian media, it can also be shown that journalists have started to fulfill the role defined by Keane as an "essential device to a system of representative government" (Keane 1992, p. 116). Despite all negative judgements, steps towards democracy have been taken, even if faltering at times. It is certainly not the aim of this study to idealize the situation in Romania. Most of the factors identified by Huntington continue to impede democratization. That is why the present work analyses some teething troubles of Romanian print media.

Romanian press before and after December 1989

Before 1989: Ceausescu's court-poetry

During Nicolae Ceausescu's reign the Romanian press had the sole task of praising the "Conductator's" strength and wisdom. Swarms of journalists and writers in the role of court-poets were constantly producing new hymns of praise. Any difficulties encountered by the Romanians during the last decades of the dictatorship were silenced. There were neither reports on accidents or crimes, nor on the existence of famine. Instead, the newspapers were full of letters in which the respective senders expressed their happiness to live in a prosperous Romania. The press was strongly centralized and totally under the control of the RCP. The 1974 press law clearly stated: "The task of the press is to fight constantly for the realization of the Communist Party's politics, the highest principles of the socialist ethics and justice"

(Leonhardt 1974, p. 453). The totalitarian adulation for the president set out the path which the media was to take up.

In the Western press the informative function of a news item is central, necessitating - in theory - the strict division between opinion and information, as well as a duty to detail current affairs (Merten 1979, p. 10). In opposition to this, the Marxist-Leninist concept proclaimed the unconditioned supremacy of ideology. The informative content of a news item was not a sufficient criterion in matters of publication in Communist Romania. The press was not considered an economic enterprise, but rather an ideological instrument for the education of the population. All production costs were state-funded and the means of production were directly controlled by the RCP (Hallenberger 1994, p. 81). Once a week the editors responsible for the five national daily newspapers[2] were called to the office of the party secretary in charge in order to receive guidelines for the coming week. Representatives from television and the press agency were also present at these meetings.

Hugo Hausl, who was then chief editor of the *Neuer Weg* newspaper, explained in a later interview how complete these directives had been: "We were told where to go. In such a precise manner that Romanian newspapers had as little difference as one egg from another. The photos were pre-selected and no editor had any say" (Schuster 1992, p. 192). Journalists wrote articles with a predetermined content and title. There was no question of research, truth-content or innovation. Many journalists suffered under this censorship. They developed an ambiguous way of writing to protect themselves from ideological pressure. They hoped their readers would read between the lines. But what was still possible in the domain of literature and culture was impossible in political reporting. Only after Ceausescu's fall could Romanian journalists express what they felt, as did Edda Reichrath in the daily paper *Neuer Weg*:

We have abused our language, using a flood of superlatives, adjectives and pompous style...But we survived. Here we are, still writing. Now we are finally free to say and write what was choking us for so long...I have more enthusiasm for my work. While the shots die away, we learn to write" (personal interview 1996).

128

The aforesaid statement – "while the shots die away, we learn to write" – is typical of the euphoric mood, which prevailed in Romania directly after the revolutionary days of December 1989. In the first months after the downfall of Ceausescu the Romanian print media developed like an avalanche and became a catalyst for democratic development. A multiplicity of new publications was created, and the print runs of existing newspapers jumped to new heights.

România Libera, which had appeared before the revolution with approximately 290.000 copies, had a print run of 1.3 million in spring 1990. *Adevarul*, the former party newspaper *Scînteia*, even reached two million copies with the help of subscriptions still originating from the Communist era (Gross 1991, p. 90). The need for information and the desire to read seemed insatiable, in particular within the urban population. Reports on scandal, crimes and accidents, which did not exist at all in the Communist press, were very prominent. But the interest of the reader also extended to political and social information. At last reality and report seemed to agree, the newspapers contained criticism of the government and one could also read about the difficulties of everyday life with which everybody had to struggle. Newspapers were cheap and in general not very long (approximately four pages). In front of the kiosks there were long queues, and it was quite normal to read three to four publications a day.

By the end of 1990 these prosperous times for the Romanian print media began to change. The print runs decreased drastically, and newspaper prices rose. This was due particularly to the self-financing of newspapers determined in February 1990 by government decree, as well as to the general lifting of price controls in November of the same year, which affected the price of subsidized paper. The national paper factory *Letea* could not respond to the sudden rise in demand. First shortages, then the rise in prices, and finally paper rationing took place. During the first 'paper crisis' in April 1990, when the presidential campaign was taking place, many newspapers had to reduce their content (Schuster 1992, p. 50), or could not organize it as they wished (e.g. *România Libera*). Due to the lack of paper, some of the daily papers were forced to suppress one edition per week.

Since 1991 economic difficulties have continued to affect the development of the written press. Many publications - experts estimated a total number of 1,600[3] - appeared in Romania in such small numbers that they survived only through the financial assistance of rich business people. Above all weekly papers and smaller newspapers have already ceased to print. Others fight for survival, sometimes at the expense of their editorial liberty and balance. In the meantime, the polarization of the press landscape has taken place. Equally, the development of an often emotional and aggressive style further contributes to a notable loss of credibility. Moreover, smaller newspapers work unprofessionally with scarcely any access to sources of detailed information. Thus, it frequently happens that rumors are simply spread, serving political goals.

The loss of credibility, the degradation of living standards as well as the increase in production costs and prices led to Romanian newspapers losing a major part of their influence after their initial success. According to a report from the independent sociological research center CURS in Bucharest published in July 1996, only six percent of the population obtain their political information from newspapers (Creanga 1996). In spite of this finding, certain topics - above all corruption affairs - are only revealed because of their appearance in the written press, sometimes even resulting in the offender being taken to court. In short, "newspapers still dominate the political discussion within the media", stated Petre Bacanu of *România Libera* (personal interview 1996).

The relationship between the government and the press in 1996

During the days of the revolution in December 1989 nearly all Romanian newspapers organized themselves as corporations and called themselves independent. Since then only cultural newspapers and publications of the national minorities have been subsidized by the government. *Vocea României*, the porte-parole of the government, and *Dimineata*, the newspaper of the presidential office, are hardly taken seriously. In recent years, most publications that have achieved economic and editorial independence often criticized the former PDSR government. In office until 1997, it was accused of hindering radical reforms, particularly economic liberalization and mass-privatization.

Within the independent written press the desire for a change of power predominated in the autumn of 1996, and the government party PDSR had a rather negative image. This was already apparent in the local elections of June 1996, in which the government party had to accept bad results, particularly in the cities, where traditionally most newspapers are read. At an extraordinary party congress of the PDSR on the 26th July 1996, the secretary general, Viorel Hrebenciuc, acknowledged that the party had not succeeded, a fact influenced by the far from perfect relationship which existed between the party and the press. Adrian Nastase, chairman of the Lower House and executive director of the party, went a step further, describing the relationship of the PDSR with the mass media as "a shambles". He also stated that this had to be improved before the upcoming general elections. At the same time he threatened "to break contact" with opposition-friendly newspapers such as *România Libera* or *Ziua*, in particular if they continued with their "dubious and reality-deforming reports". In the eyes of many journalists comprehensive political change was necessary in order to demonstrate that in a democratic system irresponsible policy-making can be criticized by an independent media, and punished through the ballot box.

Some teething problems of the Romanian press

The legislative framework

In Romania a press law does not exist, a fact which is welcomed by almost all Romanian journalists. Since 1990 several legislative initiatives have been undertaken by the Senate and/or the Lower House, but each of them have been rejected. The refusal to pass a press law is due to the fear that legislative regulation could contain restrictive provisions, which make arbitrary application possible. Distrust *vis-à-vis* legislative power and the judiciary have been strong among journalists. Adrian Ursu, head of the department for domestic affairs in the periodical *Adevarul*, explained in August 1996: "Already now, journalists have been sentenced arbitrarily. Any press-law would only provide a further instrument to the government to limit freedom of the press." At present, Romanian journalists are subject to the following laws:

1 Article 30 of the new constitution guarantees freedom of opinion and freedom of expression. Censorship is explicitly forbidden. The creation of publications is free. Existing publications may not be forbidden. At the same time, Article 30 contains a restriction on these liberties: the opinion expressed may not offend the honor or privacy of persons nor defame the state or nation. Further laws define "defamation" and "insult" (Art. 30, 8).

2 Supplementary laws have not been passed. Reforming the outdated penal code has failed twice in the Lower House and the Senate. Therefore the penal code of the Communist era, which is still in use, contains no specific references to the press. However journalists often run into trouble because of three articles:

§ 205 of the penal code refers to the "insult of any person or institution", punishable by fines and/or a prison sentence of up to three months;

§ 206 of the penal code refers to the "defamation of any person or institution", punishable by fines and/or a prison sentence of up to one year;

§ 238 of the penal code refers to the "insult or slander of authorities or public dignitaries", punished by fines and/or a prison sentence of up to three years. In "extreme cases" the punishment can be raised to a prison sentence of up to five years. Unfortunately there is no clear explanation as to what is to be considered an "extreme case". Romanian lawyers, for example the judge Corneliu Turianu, have attacked this article because it seems to define two categories of Romanian citizens: those who may not be criticized, a kind of Orwellian "some [animals] are more equal than others", and the rest of the citizenry.

3   The *European Convention for Human Rights* is valid in Romania. The Romanian parliament ratified this convention in 1994 (Monitor 1994). Article 10 of the European Convention guarantees liberty of opinion and the right to free expression.

4   Article 31 of the Romanian Constitution embodies the right of every citizen to information. But two laws discussed since 1995 (law on state secrets and law on trade secrets) endanger the unhindered access to information for the press.

Since 1990 some legal cases have shown that Romanian courts do not always interpret the penal code in favor of journalists.[4] A reform of the penal code seems urgent. It will be one of the most important duties of the new Ciorba government[5] to modernize legislation in general, and particularly the penal code. Romanian journalists hope that this reform will not be similar to the last one proposed by the Chamber of Deputies in autumn 1995. This version did not fundamentally change the character of Articles 205, 206 and 238. It only included a special paragraph referring to the press and introduced longer punishments. The Romanian media protested vigorously against these proposals and the legislative project had to be abandoned.

Continuous efforts of all democratic forces in Romania are thus necessary to ensure that changes in legislation result in a legal framework which guarantees freedom of the press. Emil Constantinescu, the new president of Romania since 1997, has repeatedly underlined this fact. But even so other peril for the media arises from the economic development of the past years.

Commercial difficulties of the press

Most Romanian newspapers face dire economic problems and this is considered as the real danger for freedom of expression by almost all media experts. Advertising incomes are lower than in Western Europe.[6] Besides bureaucratic obstacles, this is probably the principal reason for Western media companies' hesitation to invest more resources in the country. Romanian newspapers find themselves in a dilemma: paper, print and distribution costs constantly rise, but the sale price must be kept as low as possible in order to be affordable for readers. Already, pensioners, unemployed people etc. simply can no longer afford the "luxury" of buying a newspaper. The dominance of national television as far as news is concerned is also a result of this economic argument. Broadcasting and television fees are low, while a daily paper costs as much as a loaf of bread. Smaller publications are often only able to survive through the financial assistance of business people or political groupings. This financial dependence has a direct impact on the freedom of expression inside editorial teams. In other words, "under the present financial circumstances the press cannot be independent", affirms Mihai Coman, present dean of the Faculty for Journalism in Bucharest (Coman 1996).

The government has a substantial influence on the economic conditions for print media in Romania. *Letea* (Bacau), the only Romanian factory for newsprint paper, is state-owned, as is the only national distribution company *Rodipet*. The government also owns *Coresi* in Bucharest, where the majority of Romanian newspapers are printed, and the press building in the north of the capital city Bucharest where almost all national newspapers have their editorial offices. After the elections of November 1996 it will be interesting to see how the new government deals with these monopoly structures. Until now, the independent press has complained again and again that the Iliescu government had used its monopoly position politically, trying to gain control over public opinion. "Special favors" from the paper mill or the printing and distribution companies can make or break a paper's existence, particularly for smaller publications.

Editors-in-chief of *Adevarul, România Libera* and other newspapers have pointed out that *Letea* (Bacau) has already stopped paper production twice, exactly during electoral campaign periods. For example during the campaign for local elections in spring 1996, when due to "modernization and technical reasons", *Letea* stopped all production for more than three months! Imported paper is more expensive and not all publications have the financial resources to buy it. Since 1990 so-called 'paper crises' have occurred at regular intervals and the "technical reasons" given do not always seem convincing. The pricing strategy operated by *Letea* also appears arbitrary. The only way to solve the paper problems of the independent press would be to abolish the state monopoly. Some efforts have already been made. *România Libera*, for example, is willing to build a second paper factory in Romania. A feasibility study has been undertaken, but the project has failed to materialize because of a lack of start-up capital (the study calculates the need for about $30 million).

In addition, many editorships are in conflict with the national distributing enterprise *Rodipet*. The most important daily papers of the country, *Adevarul* and *România Libera*, complain that *Rodipet* does not deliver their issues in time for sale. As a consequence fewer copies are sold, giving *Rodipet* a pretext to take fewer newspapers for the next distribution. *Adevarul* is only able to sell 11,000 newspapers through the national sales network of *Rodipet* (out of a total circulation of 150.000). *Rodipet* stated more copies cannot be sold. But in the Romanian provinces there might well be more demand, as the sales numbers of private distribution companies show. Publications with good links to the former Iliescu government were not affected by these problems. In addition, some allowances, e.g. reduction of VAT, special telephone tariffs etc., are customary in Western European states, but are not yet established in Romania. In fiscal terms most of the press enterprises belong to the public services sector. That means that they cannot benefit from the fiscal advantages accorded to the production sector. Since winter 1994 *Adevarul*, who had carried out a protracted lawsuit, is classified as a production enterprise. But this regulation is not transferable to all newspapers. Besides the difficulties mentioned above, the small financial resources of Romanian newspapers also restrict the access to information, especially to international news agencies and the employment of foreign correspondents.

Sources of information

Concerning the reporting on international events, the information given by international news agencies (such as *AFP, DPA, Reuters*, etc.) is all the more important, because no Romanian newspaper has any correspondents abroad. All editors affirmed that their respective paper could not afford the costs. Romanian newspapers concentrate on domestic politics and events. Generally more than 90 percent of a daily paper is filled with information about Romania. Crossing the border still seems to be difficult. But access to domestic information often represents a problem for Romanian journalism, especially for smaller publications. As far as the political administration is concerned, there does not exist any legal obligation, as in the German press law, to inform the press. During a public round-table discussion about the press in February 1996, Petre Bacanu, editor-in-chief of *România Libera*, described the daily fight for information as follows: "Here in Romania almost all information is either stolen, or bought, or simply invented". Unfortunately many ministries have maintained a piece of Communist mentality: they refuse to publish any information. The majority of domestic information processed by Romanian journalists originates from 'unofficial sources', i.e. indiscretions from personally known informants. The kind of information they deliver may often appear exciting, but it can hardly be verified. Therefore the well-known 'golden rule' of Western journalism, not to publish any news without corroboration from a second, independent source, cannot yet be respected in Romania.

Since 1989 several private news agencies have emerged and the former Communist monopoly *Agerpress* has become *Rompres*. The situation of Romanian news agencies has improved in recent years but still suffers from various defects. For example, in the eyes of many Romanian journalists, *Rompres* does not offer enough investigative or critical material, and the style has not changed much since the Communist era. All investigative editorial crews therefore prefer *Mediafax*, the most important Romanian agency created after 1989. But *Rompres* still has the most extensive national network of journalists. Since the 1990 revolution some regional agencies have also developed, such as *ASIS Iasi*. But because of financial problems, they cover only small areas. Many of the newly created agencies pay very low salaries, and as a consequence professional full-time journalists are rarely employed.

Romanian journalists and journalistic standards

Approximately 12.000 professional journalists are currently employed in Romania, most of whom are very young. Nearly all work as a permanent member of staff because free-lance journalism does not exist. The incomes of journalists working in the print media are generally above the national average, which was about 200,000 Lei in August 1996. However, salaries can vary greatly according to the different publications as well as to the hierarchic level achieved within the editorship. Of the major national daily papers *Adevarul* payed the highest wages in August 1996 (600,000 Lei). Journalists of *România Libera* earn less (400,000 Lei). During an interview in August 1996, the editor-in-chief of *România Libera* commented ironically on this fact: "People who work for us must be idealists".

Usually all newspapers pay low wages. Journalists earn about half of their money as a fixed wage, the rest depending on the length of their published articles. This wage system has been invented to "motivate" the journalists to write as much and as rapidly as possible. However, the lower fixed wages are, the stronger this "motivation strategy" has the unpleasant side effect of extreme competition. Journalism becomes a real "struggle for life", forcing Romanian journalists to engage in all kinds of intrigues against colleagues. As a result, the quality of reporting is often reduced and many rumors and intrigues are published without any verification. Changing the wage-system would probably improve both the situation of every journalist as an individual person, as well as the general quality of the Romanian press. Unfortunately the existing interest organizations of journalists, which could fight for a change of the wage system (like AZR, UZPR, SZR, APT and APS) do not have much impact.

Another important characteristic of Romanian journalists is the way they define their role in society. Since the revolution, journalists within the print media understand themselves above all as a kind of intellectual avant-garde, fighting for the installation of a new political order. This has certainly had some positive consequences during the last few years. The press has become a sort of catalyst for democratization in Romania. But today it is time to adopt a more distant, objective way of reporting. According to Emil Hurezeanu, one of the most famous Romanian journalists who worked for *Radio Free Europe* during the Ceausescu dictatorship, "the press should offer more cool-blooded analysis and less emphatic political declarations". In fact, the emotional manner of writing endangers the reliability of the Romanian press. Mihai Coman, dean of the Faculty for Journalism in Bucharest, describes the present Romanian journalist as a "fighter" who feels obliged to have ideological values. Willing to build up public opinion, he/she mixes opinion and information. Objectivity has no superior importance. In a paradoxical way, former Communist journalists and the younger generation of writers join each other in publishing propaganda (Hallenberger et. al 1994, p. 83).

The idea that journalists should only report on, and not take part in, politics is predominant in Western editorships. But in Romania this concept does not find many adherents. In 1965 Emil Dovifat, 'father of modern German journalism', defined the separation of opinion from facts as the "basic rule" of democratic journalism (Merten 1979, p. 294). In comparison to this, the content analysis of *Adevarul* and *România Libera* - carried out by the author between September and December 1996 - showed that Romanian news items tend to be subjective and opinionated. Between 17 percent (*Adevarul*) and 38 percent (*România Libera*) of the articles, which were declared as "objective information", contained implicit comment.

All editors-in-chief interviewed on this topic declared that they would like to write in a more objective way, but they were obliged to respect the "taste" of Romanian readers, who would not buy a "Western" newspaper. It is true that during the dictatorship Romanians became accustomed to looking for implicit comment behind every article. Decades of Communist propaganda have formed and promoted this mentality. Today, opinion-driven information is still predominant. However, it would be an important step on the path towards democratic journalism in Romania, if journalists could reconsider their 'role of avant-garde', and start promoting the separation of message from opinion.

Romanian journalists are extremely heterogeneous as far as vocational training is concerned. "Remarkable personalities meet cultural swindlers, talented people as well as such without any vocation and, which is the most dangerous fact, professionally competent people meet those who are completely incapable" (Hallenberger et. al 1994, p. 96). The majority of Romanian journalists presently active started their professional career after the December 1989 revolution with the motto "learning by doing". Few journalists had any training, although some took short journalistic courses or weekend seminars. Only a small minority has had specific journalistic training. This is now changing as some universities and private institutes have established training programmes. The Universities of *Bucharest, Temeswar* and *Sibiu* each include a Faculty of Journalism. Communication sciences can also be studied at the Universities of *Cluj Napoca* and *Iasi*. The journalist trade union AZR has established a training institute in Bucharest where the first generation of young journalists graduated after a two-year course in August 1996. However, due to the strong polarization of opinions it is currently improbable that the media guild will establish a common institution of self regulation, like the *Presserat*, press council, in Germany. All journalists admit in theory the need for such an institution. Nevertheless every editor-in chief interviewed blamed other publications for making any co-operation impossible. Thus, it seems that it will take years before the lost confidence of Romanian readers in the press is recovered (Coman and Gross 1994, p. 224).

In order to show how and to which extent the teething problems mentioned above can influence the development of Romanian newspapers, it is useful to introduce two case studies of *Adevarul* and *România Libera*. By comparing the recent development of *Adevarul* and *România Libera* several conclusions concerning the freedom of opinion as well as the general political change in Romania will be reached.

Case studies

România Libera (Free Romania)

România Libera already appeared under the same name during the Communist dictatorship. The editorship explains not having changed the name of the newspaper after 1989 because *România Libera* had been founded in 1877, a long time before being "abused" by the RCP. According to Petre Bacanu, *România Libera* fought for freedom and democracy in the 19th century, and today's editor is willing to continue this engagement. "That's why we are proud to carry this name and we won't change it." Before 1989 *România Libera* was published by the *Front of Socialist Democracy and Unity*, a controlling body of

Communist party organizations. During Ceausescu's reign the publication was one of the five official national daily newspapers and corresponded strictly to Communist standards. Already at that time the paper was characterized by large amounts of advertising. Nowadays, *România Libera* still dominates the Romanian advertising market and as a result, the paper has greater advertising income than any other Romanian newspaper.

Before 1989 the newspaper did not show any dissident tendencies. Nevertheless, many members of today's *România Libera* claim to have worked secretly against Ceausescu even before his fall. Of course many of these 'resistance heroes' in fact became democratic-minded journalists only after 1989. But it cannot be denied that a small group of *România Libera's* journalists had decided in 1988 to produce an underground newspaper against Ceausescu's despotism. It was Petre Bacanu who had the idea for this daring venture. The plot was betrayed before the journalists could distribute the product, and Bacanu was condemned to a prison term of six years. The official reason for his punishment was "dealing with cars without authorization". Because no official document in 1988 would admit the existence of a conspiracy against the 'Conductator', such an accusation had to be fabricated.

Immediately after Ceausescu's fall in December 1989, Bacanu was set free. He became editor-in-chief of the new *România Libera* and the newspaper quickly developed into the most important forum for the Romanian opposition. However, Bacanu argued that the December uprising had been abused to hide a simple putsch inside the RCP. "The revolution has been an artificial production, aimed to lend legitimacy to the new, old-fashioned rulers" (Neue Zürcher Zeitung 1991). Basil Stefan, current director of the foreign affairs section of *România Libera*, asserts: "These people wanted Perestroyka, their aim was not at all democracy." In spring 1990, the journalists of *România Libera* were the first to use the new legislative possibilities by changing the paper into a private, independent joint-stock company. The editorship as well as the technical and administrative personnel became shareholders of the new *România Libera*, thereby preventing direct control by the government. Today the editorship owns 52 percent of the shares, the rest is owned by a British consortium (24 percent), two Romanian enterprises (*Rom Mega Vision* 11 percent and *Ana Electronic* 6 percent respectively) as well as a Romanian bank. Since 1995, the joint-stock company *România Libera* has paid out dividends to its shareholders.

Immediately after the 1989 revolution, *România Libera* attacked the new rulers in Bucharest, accusing them of being "hidden Communists". The government reacted with more or less visible repression. The state-owned paper factory *Letea* refused to supply more paper to the successful newspaper, the state-owned printers *Coresi* claimed not to be able to print any additional copies, and the national distribution company *Rodipet* threw copies of *România Libera* out of moving trains. When President Ion Iliescu called the miners to Bucharest in Summer 1990 in order to "re-establish order in the capital", the editorial offices of *România Libera* were devastated. Journalists were beaten and insulted because of their "ingratitude and unfaithfulness" towards the government (Report of the International Helsinki Federation 1994, p. 13-20).

> In the first two years the government tried everything to fight against us, explains Petre Bacanu. But we resisted economic and psychological pressure as well as brutal force. Today, we are a free newspaper and we must not feel afraid of anybody or anything. In fact, the reprisals even did us a favor, because from one day to another we became famous, and even if it was a sad fame we received assistance from foreign countries: funds from the USA, printing machines from Switzerland and the Netherlands etc. (personal interview 1996).

Indeed today *România Libera* must not fear external pressure. Due to their substantial share of the advertising market, the paper has a sound financial base. Being able to buy imported paper, the publication does not depend on *Letea*. The production is independent of government facilities, and distribution is organized by private regional companies. In summer 1996, the newspaper started the construction of its own press building in the *Strada Felix* in Bucharest. But the paper has to be aware of another danger, coming from within. This active stance against governments in office since 1989 threatens to diminish the publication's quality. "We led an election campaign for six years" admitted the editor-in chief in an interview. It is clear that the paper's active opposition to Iliescu, the PDSR and the government had negative consequences on the credibility of *România Libera*. For years, information which criticized the opposition was simply not published.

The content analysis of *România Libera* shows how predominant opinion-driven information still is. The analysis of all the headlines over a two-month period showed an extremely high percentage of associative elements such as question-marks, exclamation-marks and superlatives). 57.9 percent of the headings contained such associative elements. The question is, how *România Libera*, having been faithful to the *Democratic Convention* for years, will now deal with the new government elected in November 1996. Will the former opposition paper become a kind of government publication? Another danger could be the tabloid style, introduced three years ago, following the example of the very successful newspaper *Evenimentul Zilei* ('Event of the Day'). In 1993, *România Libera*'s circulation was falling every week and as a reaction the editorship decided to adopt "modern taste". In order to increase circulation, the paper started to integrate sensationalism and a more emotional way of writing. Some journalists could not get accustomed to this new style and left *România Libera*, but according to today's director these conflicts have been "necessary and useful". "We must sell in order to survive", explained the director of foreign affairs Basil Stefan, "Therefore we also publish some spicy jokes besides the political information." (personal interview 1996). The other Romanian daily newspaper, *Adevarul*, refuses to introduce such tabloid-journalism.

Adevarul (The Truth)

In 1994, the plenary assembly of the *Adevarul*-editorship approved new statutes for the periodical. *Adevarul* is the only nationwide Romanian daily newspaper with a written statute. It is stated that *Adevarul* appeared for the first time on 25th December 1989, directly after the Romanian revolution. Besides, in the heading of every edition of *Adevarul* one can read that the newspaper was founded in 1888. The name *Scîntea* ('The Spark') does not figure anywhere, just as if it had never existed. But it is a fact that today's *Adevarul* arose from *Scîntea*, the former publication of the RCP. During the dictatorship *Scîntea* was the most important daily newspaper in the country, practicing propaganda for decades. In order to "educate the new mankind", this publication was one of the main factors responsible for the enormous distortion of reality in Communist Romania. The editorship of *Adevarul* now denies any responsibility or relationship to this entrenched legacy.

Indeed the new publication has almost nothing in common with the former Communist instrument of propaganda. In the domestic affairs department only one journalist from 1989 remains. Most of the journalists arrived after the revolution. The average age is about 30, indicating the renewal, although today's editor-in-chief, Dumitru Tinu, was previously a journalist for the *Scîntea* department of international affairs. During the past three years, *Adevarul* has become a professional and high-quality newspaper, respected abroad as well as by its competitors such as *România Libera*. Among the Romanian newspapers *Adevarul* can be said to be the most Western-styled and independent publication.

Nevertheless, the separation between information and comment is not completely respected. The content analysis shows that 17 percent of the articles designated as "pure fact" contained implicit comment. The percentage of associative elements in headings is also noteworthy (31.4 percent), showing that *Adevarul* remains in part an opinion-driven newspaper. But Dumitru Tinu claims that this is only due to a "cultural attitude" of Romanian readers. "We do not have anything more in common with *Scîntea*. We did not inherit any materials, nor money or mentality. We just lodge in the same editorial offices." If this statement applies to the current *Adevarul*, it has certainly not always been true since 1989. In the first years after the revolution *Adevarul* remained closely associated with the ruling powers in Bucharest, reporting with great sympathy on all the activities of Ion Iliescu and the *Front for National Salvation*. Eye witnesses describe that in Summer 1990, as miners occupied and devastated the offices of *România Libera*, journalists of *Adevarul* applauded from their windows on the other side of the press building.

The paper remained state-owned until May 1991, while *România Libera* became a private enterprise a full year earlier. The *Adevarul*-editorship then decided to take the first steps towards independence by organizing the paper as a private joint-stock company. Petre Roman,

Prime Minister at that time, was against this development. He wanted the newspaper to continue its close co-operation with the government. However in a general meeting the journalists voted for *Adevarul*'s new beginning. Today, *Adevarul* is a private joint-stock company, and the newspaper is considered by many Romanians as the best national daily publication. The editor's offices are still in the press building at *Piata Presei Libere* and the paper is printed in the state-owned *Coresi* company. However, editorial independence has progressed. Even before Ion Iliescu and the PDSR lost the elections in 1996, many comments in *Adevarul* criticized the government. Contrary to *România Libera*, *Adevarul* never became a politically committed paper. In the publication's statutes it is explicitly forbidden for any journalist of *Adevarul* to be a member of a political party. "This is certainly an unusual and maybe even an undemocratic step", declares the editor-in-chief, "but we wanted to make sure that our paper could not be influenced by any political power in the country. Perhaps we will abolish this regulation in a few years, but meanwhile it seems to be useful."

A special characteristic of *Adevarul* reporting is the pronounced stance against corruption. Some acts of corruption have been discovered and legal action brought by the journalists. But even when describing scandalous affairs the style of reporting still remains relatively calm and objective. In this respect, the paper clearly differs from other Romanian publications, especially from *România Libera*. The editorship of *Adevarul* opted for a more detached style, rejecting tabloid journalism. The success of the paper today seems to corroborate this decision. In August 1995, *Adevarul* had the highest circulation (about 150,000) of all Romanian daily newspapers. A further phenomenon is the fact that *Adevarul* again became an opposition paper. Critical remarks against the government published by *Adevarul* had more impact on public opinion than large headlines in *România Libera* because Romanian readers considered *Adevarul* as a more objective newspaper. Adrian Ursu, director of the domestic affairs department, recalls having been asked several times by the former Prime Minister Vacaroiu to temper justice with mercy: "He said that every critical word in our paper hurt him more than pages of insults in *România Libera*" (personal interview 1996).

The credibility that *Adevarul* acquired is also reflected in the positive development of its subscription numbers. Approximately 76 percent of the total circulation is distributed to subscribers and the number is rising. This large percentage of subscriptions is unique in the Romanian press landscape and can no longer be explained by the fact that *Adevarul* inherited the subscriptions from the Communist *Scîntea* in 1989. It thus remains to be seen how the growth of the paper will be influenced by the arrival of a new government in Bucharest. *Adevarul* does not have a well developed relationships with the ruling *Democratic Convention* as *România Libera* does. But this could in fact represent an advantage as far as independence and objective reporting are concerned.

Conclusions

The development of *Adevarul* and *România Libera* highlight that from 1989 to 1996 Romanian print media have developed in an irreversible way. They became a "mediator between citizens and their state institutions" (Keane 1992). Journalists played the role of opinion-leaders, promoting democracy and forming a nucleus of Romanian civil society. The influence of the political leadership diminished, even if that was not always the stated aim. Mihai Creanga, a Romanian journalist within *România Libera*, stated for example: "If on the one hand we must no longer be afraid of governmental oppression, we have on the other hand to be aware of our proper recklessness" (Creanga 1996, p. VII). This quotation may sounds pessimistic, but it shows that first steps towards overcoming the teething problems of the Romanian press are taking place.

However, the situation of the Romanian print media needs to be improved. Freedom of the press is at threat both from external pressures and own shortcomings. As far as legislation is concerned, the reform of the Communist penal code has to assure freedom of expression for journalists (clarification of § 205 and 206, abolishment of § 238, see page 132). The laws for the protection of state and company secrets should be lifted or reformulated, given the fact that they currently endanger communication between journalists and state officials. Also, the statutes of the public service, announced for years, should finally come into play, containing the obligation for public administration to inform the press. Finally, an anti-monopoly law should be worked out in order to prohibit the monopoly of the state over the production of newsprint paper and distribution.

The economic situation of the press in Romania could be improved by lowering import duties on paper and print machinery. A positive impact, especially for the regional newspapers, could also be reached by reducing local taxes, or implementing a single procedure for their regulation. These local taxes are often fixed in an arbitrary way. The press should be classified as part of the production sector. This would mean that publications could rely on tax benefits during the first difficult years following foundation. One could also establish privileges for the print media, such as reduced fees for mailing, transport, telephone and fax. Keane designated the "preferential treatment" of *El Pais* in Spain a few months after Franco's death as "necessary" for democratic development (Keane 1992, p. 121). Another important aspect concerns extending cooperation with Western European newspapers. Romania is a "black hole" on the journalistic map, as an editor of the German daily *Süddeutsche Zeitung* stated (personal interview 1996). Only a few Western journalists know this country, let alone cover it directly through permanently assigned representatives.

The plurality of the press as well as their capacity to criticize and the independence that several publications have achieved prove that they are becoming pillars of a new democratic society in Romania. Reporting in the lead-up to the parliamentary and presidential elections of November 1996 showed that a majority of the press is aware of its information responsibility (Gabany 1996). But freedom of the press is nowhere gained once and for ever. Following Keane's definition of democracy as "a system of procedural rules with pluralistic implications" (Keane 1992, p. 124), everything in a democratic system is in endless motion. Freedom of the press is in this sense an ongoing project which has to be realized every day and which "constantly generates new constellations of dilemmas and contradiction" (ibid., p. 129). The Romanian population is now curious to see how the new President Emil Constantinescu is going to deal with these challenges. One can only hope that the new leadership will comply with the promises, and show its commitment to freedom of opinion and to sustained independence for the media in Romania.

Notes

1   Field research was carried out by the author in Bucharest between February and August 1996. Interviews were conducted with Petre Mihai Bacanu, editor of *România Libera*, Dumitru Tinu, editor of *Adevarul*, and Emmerich Reichrath, editor of *Allgemeine Deutsche Zeitung*. Additional interviews took place with Adrian Ursu, *Adevarul's* representative for domestic affairs, and Bazil Stefan, *România Libera's* representative for foreign affairs. Furthermore, the opportunity to discuss media politics with Emil Constantinescu, currently President of Romania, and Victor Ciorbea, Prime Minister until March 1998, arose in the course of the author's stay in the country. Where indicated in the text, such quotations will be marked as 'personal interview 1996'.

2   Before 1989 those newspapers were: *Scînteia* (today *Adevarul*), *România Libera*, *Tineretul Liber*, *Neuer Weg* (today *Allgemeine Deutsche Zeitung für Rumänien*), and the Hungarian daily paper.

3   In 1992 the National Statistic Commission claimed the existence of 1.545 periodicals.

4   For example the case of Radu Mazare and Constantin Cumpana in Constanta in July 1996 (See *Adevarul* 14.07.96, p.1). Another well known case is the chief-editor of *Ziua*, accused of having offended the former President Ion Iliescu (Reporters 1995).

5   The government of Prime Minister Victor Ciorba came to office in November 1996 amid high hopes of reforms. His resignation in March 1998 followed a ruling coalition that was viciously fractious, unable to agree the 1998 budget and inept at selling big state assets. Ciorba's successor, Radu Vasile, also comes from the ruling *Christian Democrat National Peasants' Party*.

6   Advertising income represents 30 percent of total revenue for *Adevarul*.

References

Coman, M. (1996), '22', No. 24, 6.03.1996, p. II.

Coman, M. and Gross, P. (1994), 'The 1992 Presidential/Parlamentary Elections in Romania's Largest Circulation Dailies and Weeklies', *Gazette*, Vol. 52, No. 3, pp. 222-240.

Connors, S., Rhodes, M. and Warshaw, M. (1995), 'Government and Media - Differing Views on Government Control', *Transition*, Vol. I., No. 18, OMRI: Praha.

Creanga, M. (1996), 'Deturnarea libertatii presei din interiorul presei', '22', No. 24, Bucharest, page VII.

Diamond, L. and Plattner, M. (1993), *The Global Resurgence of Democracy*, St. Martin's Press: Baltimore and London.

Donsbach, W., Jarren, O., Kepplinger, H. and Pfetsch, B. (1993), *Beziehungsspiele - Medien und Politik in der öffentlichen Diskussion*, Verlag Bertelsmann Stiftung: Gütersloh.

Gabanyi, A. U. (1990), *Die unvollendete Revolution*, Piper: München.

----, (1996), 'Kommunalwahlen in Rumänien', *Südosteuropa*, Vol. 45, No. 11-12, pp. 781-815.

Gross, P. (1991), 'Rumäniens Massenmedien: Neue Vielzahl und ungewisse Zukunft', *Media Perspectives*, No. 2, pp. 90-95.

Hallenberger, G. and Krzeminski, M. (1994/eds.), *Osteuropa - Medienlandschaft im Umbruch*, Vistas-Verlag: Berlin.

Huntington, S. (1991), *The Third Wave*, Oklahoma Press: Norman and London.

----, (1993), 'The Clash of Civilizations?', *Foreign Affairs*, Vol. 72, No. 3.

International Helsinki Federation for Human Rights (1994), *Human Rights in Romania After Ceausescu*, Vienna.

Ionescu, D. (1995), 'Big Brother is Still Watching', *Transition*, Vol. I, No. 10, OMRI: Praha.

Keane, J. (1992), 'Democracy and the Media', *Political Studies*, Vol. XL, special issue, pp. 116-130.

Leonhardt, P. (1974), 'Rumänien - Das rumänische Pressegesetz von 1974', *Jahrbuch für Ostrecht*, Vol. XV, No. 1 and 2, München.

----, (1992), 'Rumänien - Die neue Verfassung von 1991', *Jahrbuch für Ostrecht*, Vol. XXXIII, No. 1, München.

Melescanu, T. (1996), 'Romania's Option for the European and Atlantic Integration', *Südosteuropa*, Vol. 45, No. 11-12, pp. 773-781.

Merkel, W. (1994), 'Systemwechsel: Probleme der demokratischen Konsolidierung in Ostmitteleuropa', *Aus Politik und Zeitgeschichte*, B 18-19/94, 6 May 1994, Bonn.

Merten, K. (1979), *Struktur der Berichterstattung der deutschen Tagespresse. Eine repräsentative Inhaltsanalyse der Tagespresse der Bundesrepublik Deutschland*, Klasius: Bielefeld.

Monitor Oficial (1994), *Law 30/1994*, 31.05.1994, No. 135, Bucharest.

Mungiu, A. (1995), *Românii Dupa '89 - Istoria unei neîntelegere*, Humanitas: Bucuresti.

Neue Züricher Zeitung, 04.12.1991.

Oschlies, W. (1994), 'Wirtschaftsreform und Reformdebatten in Rumänien', *Berichte des Bundesinstituts für ostwissenschaftliche Studien*, No. 42, Köln.

Nelson, D. (1992), *Romania After Tyranny*, Westview Press: Boulder and Oxford.

Patapievici, I. (1996), *Politice*, Humanitas: Bucuresti.

Reporters Sans Frontieres (1995), *La liberté de la presse dans le monde, Report des activités*, chapter on Romania, Paris.

Rhodes, A. (1996), 'The Role of Civil Society in Support of a Stable Democratic Security Order', *Romanian Journal of International Affairs*, Vol. 2, No. 3, p. 143.

Schuster, E. (1992), *Vom Huldigungstelegramm zur Information*, Universitätsverlag Brockmeyer: Bochum.

Sparks, C. (1992), 'The Press, the Market and Democracy', *Journal of Communication*, Vol. 42, No.1, pp. 36-51.

Stamenov, S. (1993), 'Media in Romania - Special Focus', *Balkan Media*, Vol. I, No. 4.

Tuculeanu, A. (1995), 'Coordonatele Juridice Ale Raspunderii Jurnalistilor', *Dreptul*, Anul VI, Seria a III-a, No.10-11, Bucuresti.

Weidenfeld, W. (1995/ed.), *Mittel- und Osteuropa auf dem Weg in die Europäische Union*, Verlag Bertelsmann Stiftung: Gütersloh.

7 Development trends and economic policy-making in Poland

Piotr Jaworski and Ryszard Rapacki

Macro- and micro-economic trends

Despite the summer floods in 1997 the Polish economy grew at a high rate. The majority of macroeconomic indicators improved, sometimes even exceeding levels forecast by international organizations or targeted in the state budget. The best examples are gross domestic product, expanding faster than the 4.1 percent[1] estimated by international organizations, or inflation being 0.1 lower than assumed in the state budget. Value added in industry in 1997 continued to grow at an even higher rate than in 1996 (9.7 percent and 7.1 percent respectively). The growing economy positively influenced the labour market, where the unemployment rate decreased. The high growth rate was also accompanied by a high increase in real wages and benefits. The growth of personal consumption resulting from this hike was lower than in 1996, while the share of savings increased. The increase in investment was three times higher than GDP expansion. As the domestic economy was not able to fully meet the demand, the gap between commodity exports and imports continued to widen and the overall current account further deteriorated. The budget deficit was again well below the planned targets, while public debt continued to remain under the Maastricht ceiling. Although the number of privatized enterprises was lower than in 1996 budget revenues resulting from SOE divestiture were higher than in 1996. Simultaneously, favourable tendencies in structural factors could be noted, namely the beginning of pension and health care reforms. Let us now look at the evolution of economic trends in more detail.

For the first time in the past twenty-five years Poland's growth of *gross domestic product* in 1997 – registered at 6.9 percent - was higher than that of the world's fastest expanding region, South East Asia. In this region GDP on average rose only by 6.8 percent, i.e. the lowest figure for the last seven years. Poland also had one of the highest rates in Europe, the only two countries with a higher GDP growth in 1997 were Estonia and Belarus. The high increase of Poland's GDP was caused by rapid growth of value added in industry - 9.7 percent, and in construction - 17.6 percent (as compared to 3.5 percent in 1996). In terms of US dollars (based on the official exchange rate) total Polish GDP in 1997 amounted to some US$ 134.5 billion, i.e. US$ 3,500 *per capita*. If purchasing power parity is applied the figure for 1997 rises to some US$ 7,000 (Kowalik 1998). This is equivalent to 37 percent of the average Western European level (15 percent - if the official rate of exchange is adopted). How can this impressive performance of a post-communist economy in transition be explained?

Let us start with the demand side of Poland's economy. If we look at the composition of *aggregate demand* in 1997 we can see that domestic absorption, i.e. investment and consumer spending, played a very important role as an engine of Poland's GDP growth. Its expansion was lower than in 1996 (7.5 percent and 6 percent respectively). A favourable tendency can equally be observed in investment, where spending rose by 24 percent in real terms (25 percent on gross fixed investment). 1997 also registered a further upward trend in *real income*. They rose by 7.2 percent, while in 1996 the increase amounted to 4.8 percent. Real wages rose by 9.2 percent, while social security payments appreciated by 4.4 percent. The replacement ratio of pensions to wages amounted to 61 percent. A stabilising trend can be observed here: in 1996 this stood at 61.2 percent, in 1995 it reached 63.5 percent, and for 1994 the figure was 64.0 percent. This development, together with plans for pension reform (see Bastian, chapter 4 in this volume), gives further hope for an increase in household savings. On the other hand, with real wages being higher than GNP growth, together with an expansion in consumer spending, pressures on inflation and the trade balance are pronounced. The net effect of last two factors, i.e. whether extra wages fuel investment or exasperate inflation and the trade deficit, depends on their relative strength. In spite of growing domestic absorption positive trends can be observed. In the second part of 1997 the difference between the dynamics of GDP growth and domestic absorption diminished. This decreased the danger of the Polish economy overheating.

Table 12

Macro-economic indicators in Poland, 1991-97 (in percent)

Item	1991	1992	1993	1994	1995	1996	1997
Real GDP	-7.0	2.6	3.8	5.2	7.0	6.1	6.9
Consumption	7.5	3.5	4.6	3.9	4.1	7.2	7.0
Gross fixed Investment	-4.5	2.8	2.9	9.2	18.5	21.6	25.0
Government Spending	-26.6	10.4	-2.8	3.7	3.6	2.5	1.6
Export revenues*	-1.7	10.8	1.0	20.5	16.7	6.3	6.4
Industrial output	-11.9	2.8	6.4	12.1	9.7	8.5	10.8
Agricultural output	-1.6	-12.7	6.8	-9.3	10.7	0.7	-0.1
Unemployment	11.8	13.6	16.4	16.0	14.9	13.2	10.5
Budget deficit	3.8	6.0	2.8	2.7	2.7	2.5	1.6
CPI	70.0	43.0	35.3	32.2	27.8	19.9	14.9
Gross profit Margin*	4.6	2.1	2.8	4.1	4.8	3.8	3.9

* January – November for the years 1995-97.
Source: GUS (1998).

The dynamics of the Polish economy draw attention to a challenging question: Is a Czech-style currency and current account crises likely under the present conditions? The Polish government's awareness of the challenge and the measures undertaken in its 1998 budget, together with Central Bank activities could prevent it. Also, the institutional changes

Central Bank activities could prevent it. Also, the institutional changes in the Polish economy, particularly the degree of real privatization, can be seen as a decisive factor. During 1997 the weight of the private sector in the Polish economy further increased. Its share in total employment rose from 65.1 percent in 1996 to 68.9 percent (in terms of GDP 60 percent in 1996 and 58 percent in 1995). Furthermore, 22.671 new private firms were created (a 9.5 percent increase). The level of short-term foreign debt and hard currency reserves also contributed to support our hypothesis. They reached almost US$ 4 and 20 billion respectively.

The *investment/GDP ratio* further augmented from 18.5 percent in 1996 to 21.4 percent in 1997 (1995: 17.1 percent). This, together with the increase of household savings' share in disposable incomes, is a favourable trend. If it can be sustained all the better. However, the share of investment in GDP as well as the share of household savings in disposable income is still much lower than in other European countries. Comparing the private and public sector, growth of investment outlays in the former reached 76 percent (in nominal terms), while in the latter it amounted to only 10 percent. As a result, the share of the private sector in total investment rose from 41 percent in 1996 to 52 percent last year. In the composition of investment the share of manufacturing decreased from 60.1 percent in 1996 to 54.2 percent last year, whereas the share of services as well as post and telecommunications increased (from 7.4 percent to 8.8 percent, and 7.2 percent to 9.1 percent respectively). The strongest dynamic of investment was recorded in timber and the automobile industry, while the investment in coal, brown coal and metallurgy decreased. 35 percent of private sector investment originated from firms controlled by foreign capital (with an equity stake over 50 percent).

In 1997 *exports* again increased slower than *imports*. As a result the external balance of the Polish economy further deteriorated. However, the difference between the dynamics of imports and exports diminished during 1997. In the fourth quarter exports together with trans-border trade were 15 percent higher than in the same period of 1996. A similar trend could be observed in imports. In the fourth quarter of 1997 they rose by 19 percent, whereas in the same period of 1996 they amounted to 24 percent. This development gave rise to a deficit in both trade and current accounts for 1997: US $10.1 billion and US $3.9

billion respectively. The current account deficit was also accelerated by a deterioration of the so-called 'unclassified current transactions' balance, which was positive, but lower than in 1996 when US $6.7 billion were recorded compared to US $5.6 billion for 1997. This trend underlines the prediction of some economists who argue that the importance of transborder trade is declining, especially when attempting to ease balance of payment pressures.

Firms controlled by foreign capital increased their exports by 71.4 percent and imports by 57.1 percent. However, due to their high propensity to import, the balance between exports and imports was negative and further deteriorated. Nevertheless, there is a positive sign for the future. Throughout 1997 the gap between the dynamics of exports and imports diminished. Another favourable trend for Polish foreign trade is a decreasing share of goods classified as raw materials in exports - from 27.5 percent in 1995 to 26.1 percent for the January - November 1997 period, while the share of industrial goods rose from 20.9 percent to 23.5 percent respectively. Furthermore, the share of investment imports increased whereas personal consumption goods decreased. However, the price relations in Polish foreign trade (January-October period) were unfavourable. The terms of trade amounted to 99.4. In the case of the European Union the figure was 101.4, and for Central-Eastern Europe 93.5.

Another aspect that is noteworthy concerns the fact that for the first time in 1997 *foreign direct investment* to Poland was higher than in Hungary. With a total of US $6.6 billion invested, Poland became the leading country on the list of FDI inflows into the region. However, the value of FDI per capita, equal to US$ 534, is still lower than in Hungary, Slovenia and the Czech Republic. 70 percent of foreign investors come from the European Union. This is also a promising factor for the Polish trade balance as there is a close relation between the origin of direct foreign capital and exports of foreign-owned firms (see Bod, chapter 2 in this volume). The two largest foreign investors, *Fiat* from Italy and *Daewoo* from South Korea, have mainly invested in the automobile industry, which is turning Poland into a regional centre for car manufacturing.

Seen from the supply side, the Polish economy in 1997 experienced a further expansion of *industrial output*. Production rose by 10.8 percent as compared to 8.3 percent in 1996. Construction has become a new engine of growth in the Polish economy. It rose by 17.6 percent in 1997 (3.5 percent in 1996). The share of private sector construction increased from 88.1 percent in 1996 to 93.2 percent in 1997. Growth in manufacturing was equally above the recorded average - 13.5 percent. Within manufacturing capital goods production rose by 16 percent, consumer durables by 13 percent, intermediate products by 13 percent, water, gas and power generation contracted by 2.6 percent, while output in the extractive industries decreased by 1.2 percent. Production growth was accompanied by an increase in labour productivity (12 percent). However, we must acknowledge that the full effects of the 1997 summer floods on the Polish economy cannot be evaluated yet. While they did not adversely affect the dynamics of growth, the floods nevertheless affected the level of capital stock. Therefore, its consequences will only be seen within a longer time perspective, and we must reserve judgement about their full consequences at this stage.

The situation on the Polish *labour market* further improved. The number of people in employment totalled 15.9 million in 1997, growing by 0.6 percent compared to 1996. In December 1997 there were 182,640 registered unemployed. In the course of 1997 the number of unemployed decreased by 22.6 percent. This significant decline was attributed to a change in classification. Those unemployed over the age of sixty years were given pre-pension benefits or underwent training. Since January 1997 they have not been treated as registered unemployed anymore. This classification change is the single most important reason behind the drop in the unemployment rate from 13.2 percent in 1996 to 10.5 percent in 1997. However, there is still a large disproportion in the unemployment rates between different regions, from 2.8 percent in the capital city Warsaw to 21.2 percent in the Suwalki *voivodship* in eastern Poland.

One of the most important achievements in 1997 was the fulfilment of the budget target for *inflation*. The consumer price index increase in 1997 was equal to 14.9 percent, 0.1 percent lower than the target in the state budget. Overall inflation, measured by the GDP deflator, amounted to 13.2 percent. The highest rise in prices was recorded in services, the lowest in food prices. Another characteristic of 1997 was the reduction of inflationary *expectations*. The prime factor responsible for this phenomenon was the meeting of the budget target for inflation. Secondly, the change in some of the indexing rules, such as pension indexation, also added to this downward trend. Furthermore, the margin of administered prices in public services and private goods provided by the state-owned sector diminished. In 1997 increases in administered prices contributed 3.5 percentage points to the overall consumer price index growth (0.5 percent less than in 1996). On the other hand, structural factors shaping inflation were not eliminated. An important issue in this regard is the attractiveness of foreign direct investment on Polish capital markets. Relatively high interest rates and confidence in the Polish economy attract short-term foreign speculative capital, thereby increasing the overall money supply.

The *budget deficit* reached 6.1 billion zloty, which constitutes half of the amount planned by the government in 1997. However, the picture is not as bright as first meets the eye. If we calculate the deficit according to new rules, which are to be applied to the 1998 budget and deficit calculation, i.e. excluding revenues from privatization, then the deficit in 1997 rises to 12.6 billion zloty. Furthermore, if we also take into consideration the overdue debt of state institutions, we should add almost 3 billion, and we thus end up with a deficit closer to 15.5 billion zloty, which constitutes almost 3.6 percent of GDP. This figure looks much less positive. The structure of government spending is not optimistic either. The share of pension subsidies rose during the past year from 6.9 percent to 7.4 percent. If this trend continues, the financial squeeze will further constrain expenditure in other areas. The share of domestic debt service in the state budget rose by 0.1 percent to 10.1 percent. In absolute terms the burden of debt servicing constitutes 2/3 of the revised deficit. On the other hand, if total public finances are considered the revenue and expenditure configuration of local governments must also be mentioned. Their consolidated financial result was positive and amounted to 1 billion zloty. In the light of decentralization plans and the introduction of the subsidiarity principle, this evolution can be treated as a positive prospect for the future rationalization of public spending.

Economic policy-making in 1997

From the political point of view the most important event in 1997 was the general election in September. The outcome brought a complete change on the political stage. In the light of pre-electoral uncertainty and possible post-election coalition options, the general direction of economic policy-making was not altogether changed. What is worth highlighting is nevertheless the fact, that the new right-of centre AWS-UW coalition government has placed more emphasis on long-term development and structural reforms, while the previous left-of centre government favoured re-distributive policies. The other goal strongly embraced by the former government was the expansion of household incomes, which in turn resulted in consumption growth described in the previous section.

The former SLD-PSL government was aware of the Czech and Hungarian crises scenarios. Hence, it prepared a rather restrictive budget for 1998, which was aimed at avoiding exorbitant current account deficits and currency volatility. The new government inherited the austerity objectives and accepted the budget outline with few amendments. The first results of this implementation, together with more restrictive fiscal policy measures, can be seen in the decline of the growth dynamic of consumption credits. The new government further declared its political will to accelerate long awaited structural reforms. Health care and social security reforms, initiated by the former government during the last phase of its term in office, were given a new impetus on the legislative agenda. Also, administrative reform of the regions, delayed for a long time, is to be implemented ahead of the 1998 local government elections. Finally, there are plans to substantially reduce bureaucratic hurdles for private firms. All these goals, if accomplished, would lay a solid basis for a self-sustained and balanced development of the Polish economy into the next century.

We start our more detailed overview with *fiscal policy-making*. As was already mentioned, the 1997 budget deficit was lower than expected. This result was achieved in spite of a long awaited lowering of tax brackets from 21, 33 and 45 percent to 20, 32 and 44 percent respectively. The former figures had been introduced in 1994 and were maintained - despite official pledges to revise them downwards -

throughout 1997. The change of tax brackets was combined with the revision of various tax deduction provisions. In order to balance the budget the outgoing government had tried to increase the efficiency of the tax collection system by introducing a new tax code that sought to facilitate the administrative procedures of tax authorities. For example, the confidentiality of taxpayers' bank accounts was to be lifted at the request of the tax authority. The new government has announced further tax reductions. As a first step it lowered the tax brackets. The figures for 1998 are now as follows: 19, 30 and 40 percent respectively. However, at the same time VAT on telecommunication services and energy sources was increased from seven to 22 percent. The instability of tax legislation, especially tax deduction provisions being changed every year, does not contribute to the creation of a sustainable incentive structure guiding the behaviour of economic agents. Such short-term approaches seeking to meet current budgetary needs characterized the former government and risks being repeated now.

In spite of a try-partite wage negotiation system it should be stressed that the *incomes policy* of the former government was rather expansionary. The target of real wages growth, 2.4 percent in 1997, established by the try-partite committee, was substantially exceeded. It led to excessive consumption growth, which in turn increased the threat of overheating the economy and further deteriorating the balance of trade. These tensions and the will to check consumer credit expansion resulted in a more restrictive policy of the *Polish Central Bank* (NBP). It increased interest rates in August 1997 by 2.5 percentage points to the level of 27 percent. The NBP also started to take deposits from households at higher than commercial banks' interest rates. This brought about a lower dynamic of consumer credit, but on the other hand it could worsen the situation when the NBP deposits are requested back by costumer demand and the market will be affected by a strong inflationary stimulus. The high interest rates also attracted speculative foreign capital, which increased the pressure on the appreciation of the Polish currency and could thus contribute to a further trade balance destabilization. In order to dampen speculative capital inflows the band of exchange rate fluctuations was widened to seven percent in each direction. From 1998 onwards key monetary decisions are to be made by a new institution, the *Monetary Policy Board*, which was established in late 1997 by the outgoing government. Its creation can be seen as one more factor to mitigate inflationary expectations. Finally, in 1997 the NBP switched its monetary targets from the reserve money (M_0) level to interest rates setting.

The beginning of 1997 finally brought a long awaited restructuring of Poland's central *economic administration*. Several government agencies merged to create fewer, yet more coherent ministries, such as the Ministry of Economy and the Treasury Ministry. The underlying rationalization objective of this reform is laudable. But in practice both ministries have been divided between different political parties with divergent economic programmes in the new government coalition. This situation risks hampering the effectiveness of decision making and weakening the creation of a coherent economic policy framework. The best example for this assumption is the case of *Ursus*, Poland's biggest tractor producer, who stands on the verge of bankruptcy. It was supplied with new credits by the Treasury. This move was incompatible with government declarations about restructuring and hard budget constraints imposed on state firms.

As in previous years the *privatization* process yielded good results when assessed from the budget revenue angle. Revenues for the January-November 1997 period were 45.2 percent higher than targeted, amounting to over 6.460 million zloty. In 1997 privatization embraced 13 new enterprises, i.e. more than in 1996. On the other hand, the remaining number of SOEs was 34 percent lower than in 1996, and reaching 253 firms. Among them 18 percent were converted into joint stock companies fully owned by the state. By the end of 1997 the privatization process had comprised 5.844 SOEs, i.e. 67 percent of all existing firms since the beginning of the process in mid-1990. The privatization prospects are ambiguous. The *Ursus* tractor factory may again serve as an example: *AEGCO*, an American producer of agricultural machines, withdrew from a planned purchase because of lacking support from the Treasury. On the other hand, the Treasury plans to sell a 49 percent stake in LOT, the Polish airlines, to a strategic investor. However, this will require a change in legislation because present regulations only permit the sale of a 30 percent share of public utilities.

The *National Investment Funds* (NIF) programme adhered to its schedule. In June 1997 all 15 funds started to be traded on the Warsaw Stock Exchange. According to Treasury data for the January - September 1997 period the investment portfolio of NIFs reached the sum of 6.188 million zloty, of which 92 percent was constituted by the equity capital brought in at the beginning. The revenues out of NIF investment were 57 percent higher than in 1996 and amounted to 161.4 million zloty. 84 firms involved in the programme acquired outside investors, 10 were traded on the Warsaw Stock Exchange main floor, and 9 over the counter market.

It is still too early to asses the economic policy programme of the new government in full. Its main task should be to prevent the repetition of a Czech style crisis. From a long-term perspective the capability of the new government to carry out genuine market-oriented transformations can be assessed on the basis of handling a variety of challenges. After 100 days in office first symptoms of decision deadlocks within the new government can be identified. The ability to handle the problems listed below will be a test of the coalition's determination:

1. Comprehensive reform of the pay-as-you-go pension system, including the legal framework for private pension plans and pension funds (see Bastian, chapter 4 in this volume).

2. Reform of the health care funding system.

3. Demonopolization of the insurance system.

4. Investment in human capital alongside necessary reforms in education, research and development.

5. Policies towards strengthening the competitive position of the Polish banking sector.

6.   Implementation of long delayed restructuring programmes in key
      sectors of the economy, such as mining, metallurgy, power
      generation, heavy chemistry and oil-processing industries.

7.   Further acceleration of the privatization programme, including the
      possible extension of the Mass Privatisation scheme (NIF).

The Polish road towards the European Union

The year 1997 was very significant for the issue of Polish accession to
the European Union (EU). Together with Estonia, Cyprus, the Czech
Republic, Hungary and Slovenia, Poland was invited to commence
negotiations on prospective membership. Although there is still much
to be done in the process of transforming the Polish economy, this
major achievement justified the boldness of economic strategies
undertaken at the beginning of the decade. The idea of Polish EU
membership appeared at the early stages of the transformation process.
Moreover, it was recognised by *all* governments in office since 1989/90
as one of the key long-term economic and political goals. The *Europe
Agreement* (EA) signed in December 1991 established formal relations
between Poland and the EU. The agreement can be treated as a first
mutual step towards reaching the stated objective. The EA entered into
force in February 1994. The EA did not contain any firm EU obligation
nor timetable to accept Poland as a future EU member. In April 1994
Poland submitted a formal application for EU membership. This was a
natural consequence of the political decision in favour of enlargement
undertaken by EU leaders during the Copenhagen Summit in June
1993. Subsequently Poland was presented with a detailed set of
inquiries on the state of economic, political, legal and social affairs.
The responses provided created the basis for the official assessment of
Poland's adequacy to enter into formal negotiations with the EU. At the
end of this process, in the middle of 1997, Poland was invited to open
negotiations with representatives from the Commission.

    The negotiations are mired in complexities and controversy. The
critical factor is economic adaptation, the sequencing of which requires
considerable financial and organizational resources. Polish GDP per

capita in purchasing power parity constitutes only 37 percent of the West European average. The level of wages is substantially lower than in the EU. Furthermore, Polish agriculture involves almost 1/3 of the entire population and is operating according to environmental standards, which are not compatible with those of the EU. This will cause the greatest problems of fine-tuning necessary adjustments. Moreover, in geographical terms Poland constitutes the economic periphery in trade relations to the EU (El-Agra 1994). During the past eight years of transformation Poland has re-oriented its economy from the trade dependency of CMEA markets to the integration with the EU. During 1997 the share of Polish exports to the EU constituted 65.3 percent, and imports from EU countries reached 64 percent. In 1997 Poland recorded a negative trade balance of 8735.4 million US$. The only way to offset this asymmetry is to increase the inflow of FDI from the EU to Poland and to further enhance trade relations. In order not to remain a peripheral country Poland should also develop close economic relations with the countries to its East, especially with neighbouring Ukraine, Belarus and Russia. It can use the competitive advantage of knowing these countries' markets and trade customs.

The accession, however, also involves major institutional changes within the EU, the most important being CAP. The current payment and pricing system is very difficult to maintain even without the EU expanding eastwards. The following problem currently arises: Given the importance of the agricultural sector in Poland, should the country be included into the CAP scheme before the latter's reform, or should it be excluded from CAP, thus joining later when a new system has been worked out? The first option appears impossible due to the cost implications. The other alternative, however, would make Poland a second class member of the EU.

It is also interesting to take a broader view at the general atmosphere surrounding Polish accession. A European Commission survey published in March 1998 shows that 43 percent of the EU population is for Polish membership, and 34 percent against it (Bielecki 1998b). The most sceptical are the Germans. Only 29 percent of its citizens support the accession, whereas in the case of Sweden the number is 69 percent, Holland 63, Greece 59, and Finland 55 percent respectively. In the context of these figures, the most important fear expressed in every country surveyed is related to labour market implications. Only three percent of Germans are eager to grant its direct neighbour to the East unconditional access to EU labour markets. Regarding Austria and Denmark the number is six percent, and Belgium arrives at seven percent. The only country enjoying greater support from the EU population on the issue of accession is Hungary, reaching 47 percent. In spite of all these reservations there seems to be no alternative option for Poland than to join the EU. This is recognised in a bi-partisan manner between the political élites in the country. Besides, the decision to join was, as Hans Van den Broek, European Commissioner for external relations, said,

> undertaken by the Polish government and parliament. Therefore, Polish parliament needs to accept the results of negotiations. It is a misunderstanding to assume...that the EU forced Poland to join (Bielecki 1998a).

Let us now look at the issue of EU membership from an organizational perspective. The schedule of negotiations is very ambitious. The European Commission plans to screen Polish legislation until Christmas 1998. Then, from the beginning of 1999, it will start negotiations on particular conditions for the accession process. This will take another two years, so January 2001 marks the possible, 'working' date of Polish accession. The years 2001 and 2002 would then be devoted to the ratification of the accession protocols and the holding of a referendum. It is assumed that in some areas, which are easier to negotiate, such as statistics, organization of scientific research, customs policy, copyright law or audio-visual policy, the screening should be completed earlier.

The most difficult negotiations will take place in the areas sensitive for Poland as well as for the EU, albeit for opposite reasons. Poland will insist on immediately securing all four freedoms of movement within the *Single Market Programme* of the EU: (i) goods, (ii) services, (iii) capital, and (iv) labour. The first freedom is already in place due to the signing of the aforementioned *Europe Agreement*. It does not include, however, 'sensitive' issues such as steel, textiles and agricultural products, and will thus be a subject of further, and rather arduous talks. The same concerns labour market mobility as can be seen from the results of the survey on the attitude of EU citizens mentioned above. On the other hand Poland has expressed its interest to protect some areas from European competition and regulations. In particular the transitional periods would apply to environmental protection rules, agriculture and food industry, the right of foreigners to buy arable land as well as transportation and the insurance market (Wegrowska 1998).

The achievement of these priorities has been set as a target for a team of Polish negotiators. It consists of sixteen specialists plus a chief negotiator, Jan Kulakowski. He is a Pole, who in 1946, at the age of sixteen, emigrated to Belgium. He received his Ph.D. in Law and International Relations at the Catholic University of Leuven. Kulakowski is well known and respected in Brussels. From 1990 onwards he was the Polish ambassador to the European Union. The chief negotiator was chosen after a rather long procedure involving 'horse-trading'. His candidature was the result of a compromise between the two political coalition parties AWS and UW. The formal status of the chief negotiator is ambiguous. He is simultaneously a secretary of state in the Prime Minister's chancellery as well as the state secretary in the *Committee for European Integration*. Hence Kulakowski is responsible both to the Prime Minister and the head of the Committee. The Committee itself is an institution with ministerial status. As a result of this architecture the role of the Ministry of Foreign Affairs has been diminished, as it is now only a co-ordinating body. This structure of inter-locking institutions risks creating the danger of institutional overlap, highlighting efficiency deficits, and thus weakening the authority of the chief negotiator. In a word, the possibility of disagreement and misunderstanding between different institutional representatives is formidable.

Another concern is whether the chief negotiator will have enough power over ministers to implement the results of the negotiations. A final issue of concern represents the head of the *Committee for European Integration*, Ryszard Czarnecki. He is a member of the ZCHN, which forms part of the ruling AWS. The ZCHN has a tradition of being eurosceptic. Some of their MPs have voted against European integration decisions tabled by the new government, and rather aligned themselves with opposition parties, namely the PSL, in order to further a parliamentary representation *against* Polish membership in the EU (Olczyk and Pilczynski 1998). Czarnecki has been indirectly criticised by Nikolaus van der Pas, the European Union chief negotiator, for some of his statements, which impeded solutions to a number of sensitive problems (Rzeczpospolita 1998). In spite of all these problems the political will between both sides should be treated as a positive sign. There is a great chance that Poles will eventually become citizens of the European Union, possibly by the year 2004, even if this timetable includes some transitional periods. To put it simply - there is no other way, and both sides realise this.

Note

1   If not specified otherwise all statistical data are from GUS (1998).

References

El-Agra, A.M. (1994), *The Economics of the European Community*, Harvester Wheatsheaf: New York.

Bielecki, J. (1998a), *Warunki Poznamy w Nowym Roku*, Rzeczpospolita, 25 February 1998.

---- (1998b), *Najbardziej Sceptyczni sa Niemcy*, Rzeczpospolita, 17 March 1998.

GUS (1998), *Informacja Statystyczna o Sytuacji Spolecno-Gospodarczej Kraju – Rok 1997*, Warsaw, 29 January 1998.

Kowalik, A. (1998), *Kolejny Rok Szybkiego Wzrostu*, Rzeczpospolita, 26 February 1998.

Rzeczpospolita, 21 March 1998, *Negocjator Krytukuje Polskiego Ministra*.

Olczyk, E. and Pilczynski, J. (1998), *Niewygodni Euroentuzjasci I Eurosceptycy*, Rzeczpospolita, 8 April 1998.

Wegrowska, M. (1998), *W Czwartek Nominacja Jana Kulakowskiego*, Rzeczpospolita, 3 February 1998.

8 From former to post: Communist parties in Central and Eastern Europe

Jens Bastian

Introduction

At the end of 1995 former communists governed in Poland and Hungary, Bulgaria and Romania, Lithuania and Serbia, Belarus and Slovakia. The similarity of this development across Central and Eastern Europe invites drawing sweeping parallels between the aforementioned countries. But caution is rather appropriate, thereby separating hype from reality. Post-communist parties can be a melange of old communists and nationalists, a mixture of ideologically disillusioned people with those still waiting to benefit from the transition to market economies. For Western policy-makers and corporate investors arriving at an informed judgement of post-communist parties is crucial. A pragmatic understanding of a new generation of left-of-centre politicians in Central and Eastern Europe is as critical as it enhances such representatives to further engage in their objective to 'return to Europe'. The political geography of transition countries is shaped by post-communist parties, the legacies they have left behind, and the internal reform processes that they are undertaking. In a word, far from making monolithic arguments as during the Soviet era, post-communism expresses different things, appears in a variety of colors and strikes any number of contradictory attitudes.

What post-communist parties all have in common is their respective point of departure, the process of going into labor and giving birth to political organizations under the socialist or social democrat banner. The experience of initially falling from power, throwing out the old leadership and accepting multi-party elections constituted a major abandonment from Leninist principles before 1989. However, this is where the parallels end. The diversity of post-communist parties in Central and Eastern Europe reflects the varying degree to which they have kept earlier reform promises, both with regard to the party organization as well as advancing liberal democracy and a privatized market economy. Frequently the rhetoric of reform is not matched by performance as the examples in Serbia, Bulgaria, Slovakia and Belarus illustrate.

Long before 1989, ruling communist parties were an expression of and evolving to suit local conditions. Romania and former Yugoslavia exemplified the capacity to adapt and carve out a niche most explicitly. In what was erroneously seen by many Western observers as obedient departments of the Soviet Empire, communist parties were as different as the empire was diverse in historical legacies, economic conditions and cultural outlook. What unites Slobodan Milosevic in Serbia, Ion Iliescu in Romania, Vladimir Meciar in Slovakia and Gennadi Zyuganov in Russia is that they all established a more or less smooth combination of post-communism with the rhetoric of nationalism. In the course of this transition process, the new post-communist parties also offered a more bearable sequencing of change in a turbulent economic environment, they presented themselves as examples of professional government against the first wave of post-1989 dissident rulers, and had a proper party organization at their disposal.

Former communist parties have renamed themselves in many of the countries once constituting the so-called Soviet orbit. The prefixes 'former' and/or 'post' require a working definition of these organizations. Henceforth, former or post-communist parties shall be understood as parties that directly succeeded the pre-1989 ruling communist parties (including legal succession), and/or people who were members of these parties until the collapse of communism. This working definition constitutes a terminological approximation. This is all the more necessary when bearing in mind that the variety of post-communist parties is not easily covered by one comprehensive definition. In contemporary Germany for instance, the rather pejorative term *Wende-Kommunisten* (U-turn communists) is used by conservative representatives of the party political spectrum when labeling the PDS, repentant heir to the SED, who ruled East Germany for forty years until 1990 (Bastian 1995). Post-communist parties can turn into good ones and dire ones, into westward-looking democrats or despots spouting the rhetoric of ethnic cleansing. Examples for this mixture – disquieting as it is – are all around us. However, neither milder versions of post-communism nor the crude, despotic and authoritarian kind will be able to revive the old Soviet model.

As mentioned before, post-communist parties have not only achieved electoral viability, but also managed to return to power in a number of countries in Central and Eastern Europe. Furthermore, renamed former communist parties have fared much better than any of the social-democratic parties existing during the inter-war period, and for a short time, after the end of World War II. Post-communist parties' electoral resurgence has enabled them to move into the political space left vacant by the weak performance of the historical social-democratic parties. Moreover, the successful occupation of this political geography has allowed these parties to be identified with social-democratic positions. This extraordinary achievement in the course of – sometimes – only three years after the fall of communism, is best exemplified by a number of communist successor parties being admitted to the *Socialist International* (Waller et al. 1994).[1]

Equally, where the reign of 'socialists' or 'social democrats' is flourishing, another reason for this success story must be found in the failure of respectable right-wing and center-right parties to establish a footing in the new political geography of Central and Eastern Europe. With the notable exception of the Czech Republic, the opposite end of the political spectrum is a near disaster area. Liberal sects, servile church parties and remote farmer organizations, nationalists under the banner of liberal democracy as Zhirinovsky in Russia, royalists like in Romania and neofachists as in Slovakia signify the absence of a coherent version of Christian democracy or even conservative party profile. Hence, the success of post-communist parties must also be seen in relation to, and is the result of any ideological rivals failing to prosper in Central and Eastern Europe. Such rivals have yet to mount a formidable challenge to former communists, thereby greatly facilitating the latter's endeavor to rise 'from the ashes'.

If the rebirth of social democracy in East-Central Europe has hardly taken place since 1989, then the core reason for this absence must rest in reformed communist parties' capacity to fill the respective voids and push potential rivals to the sidelines. In Poland, Hungary and Bulgaria, which this contribution will focus on, historic social democratic parties are not represented in national parliaments. This choice of countries exemplifies a comparative sample that allows highlighting the diversity, complexity and possible similarities between former communist parties.

Both the SdRP in Poland and the MSZP in Hungary have not only returned to power after a rather brief interlude, but they have also done so by entering into coalition agreements. In the former case power sharing included an alliance with a well-known partner before 1989, the PSL.[2] In the latter, the renamed Hungarian socialists formed a coalition with the dissident party SZDSZ in 1994, although their parliamentary majority did not oblige them to do so. Finally, the renamed Bulgarian BSP is probably the most significant example of a former communist party that has been more years in power since 1990 than residing on the hard benches of parliamentary opposition. Only with the outcome of the recent general elections in April 1997 can it be safely argued that the BSP is starting to learn the primary rule of the democratic game: alternating between opposition and government.

The changing nature of former communist parties

When analyzing the birth of post-communist parties one has to be mindful of avoiding sweeping generalizations. Unlike their predecessors these parties are now without external sustenance. There does not exist anymore a *Pax Sovietica*. Hence the fundamentally changed contextual conditions in which post-communist parties emerged and have since operated obliges any comparative examination to consider the respective differences and highlight the historical specificities of such organizations. Having said that some similarities among our sample are striking. In the process of birth the parties:

- changed their name;
- the old leadership was thrown out;
- the Leninist party structure and ideology was scraped;
- pledge to hold multi-party elections.

These common points of departure require specification. A major difference between former Communist parties in Central and Eastern Europe consists in the avenues which these parties have taken with regard to their internal process of change and reorganization.[3] The point of departure for former Communist parties in Poland, Hungary and Bulgaria varied considerably according to two parameters: (i) was the predecessor party legally dissolved, and (ii) who inherited the substantial material resources and financial assets of the organization?

In Poland, the PZPR was officially dissolved at the last party congress in January 1990. The SdRP was subsequently founded, but did *not* register as the legal heir to the PZPR. Property and financial assets of the PZPR were nationalized through legislation. Still, leading representatives of the SdRP have repeatedly been accused of having diverted financial assets of the PZPR towards the new organization, without making the necessary declarations to fiscal authorities (FAZ 17.03.1998). Since years liquidators cannot track the whereabouts of these assets. Equally, the remaining members of the PZPR were not automatically forwarded into the newly established SdRP. Although an independent party with a considerable membership base (see figure 1 next page), the SdRP is rather peculiar as a post-communist party. At elections it does not stand on its own but is part of a wider organizational alliance, the so-called SLD. This capacity to form strategic alliances in order to pool resources and advance the parliamentary representation of left-of-center representatives is a hallmark of the SdRP.

In Hungary, the MSZMP was dissolved at its 14th party congress in October 1989. The self-liquidation of the MSZMP was far-reaching. More than 90 percent of the party assets and almost all its physical property were handed over to the state. The MSZP was created in October 1989, but instantly faced a competing claim for the political heir of the MSZMP. The *Social Democratic Party of Hungary*

(MSZDP) was established by a minority of delegates who had taken part in the dissolution of the MSZMP, but refused to take part in the European-type socialist party which the MSZP was seeking to become. This refusal reflected a historical legacy in Hungarian politics: the forced alliance of the Communists and the Social Democrats in 1948. Finally, in the case of Bulgaria the BSP was the result of a renamed, but not dissolved Communist Party. The latter's members were integrated into the new organization as well as the material property of the CPB.

Table 13
Membership in selected post-communist parties 1996

PDS	104.000
Established December 1989	Downward trend
SdRP	60.000
Established January 1990	Gradual increase
MSZP	46.000
Established October 1989	Stagnation
BSP	370.000
Established November 1989	Dramatic loses in 1997

The Bulgarian BSP, Hungarian MSZP and the Polish SdRP/SDL were obliged to provide practical policy alternatives at early stages of their transformation processes. The three parties' reintegration into the mainstream of politics and institutional responsibility was either a result of the inability of other parties in government (coalitions) to carry through parliament their respective legislative initiatives, or followed electoral victories, for the BSP and SDL in 1993, while the MSZP was voted into office in 1994. To illustrate: even before the former Communists in Poland won the elections, the then Prime Minister Hanna Suchochka (*Freedom Union Party*) could only reach a parliamentary majority for a privatization law with the help of the opposition SDL. Its own five-party coalition was so at odds with each other that Suchochka had to rely on the votes of the former Communists, thus giving them a formidable opportunity to display their new-gained legislative responsibility outside government, while post-*Solidarnosc* parties were preoccupied with fighting their own coalition partners.

The electoral comebacks - and returns to government office - by former communist parties in Poland, Hungary and Bulgaria (as exemplified in figure 2 below) were preceded by successful survival strategies in economic and administrative tiers of society. The labels ascribed to such performance, for instance 'nest-feathering practices', 'repackaging', 'fancy footwork' or 'patron-client networks', highlight the mixture of change and *élite continuity* within former communist parties.

This argument does not apply to the top leadership of these parties, but rather underlines the career mobility and ideological flexibility of its many (younger) deputies. The former had to step aside, and some were prosecuted. The latter quickly emerged as the new faces of renamed former communist parties, individuals with a shallow commitment to ideology, but good commercial ties and a knowledge of the party apparatus, its resources and clientelistic practices. This mixed bag of orientations and practices has enabled these new faces of leftist politics in Central and Eastern Europe to become part of a smooth transition into democratic institutions. Moreover, in the course of the process they have accepted and used to their advantage the new rules of the game. In doing so democratic politics and electoral competition have not jeopardized their ascendancy (Segert and Machos 1995).

Table 14
Electoral success of post-communist parties

Germany:	4.4 percent overall
PDS	19.8 percent in East Germany
October 1994	
Poland:	20.4 percent
SLD	Coalition government with PSL
September 1993	27.1 percent
September 1997	Parliamentary opposition
Hungary:	32.5 percent
MSZP	Coalition government with AFD
May 1994	
Bulgaria:	44.2 percent
BSP	Absolute majority
December 1994	22.1 percent
April 1997	Opposition benches
Russia:	21.3 percent
CPRF	Strongest party in the Duma.
December 1995	Over 6 million votes in
June 1996	Presidential elections[4]

Facing up to Central and Eastern Europe's ghosts

The manner in which post-communist parties in Central and Eastern Europe attempt to confront legacies of the past in their country's respective history is one of the most telling indicators of these organizations' willingness to reconstruct and redefine themselves. There are plenty of skeletons in the cupboard of post-communist parties, all the more since the opening of archives and the determination of individuals to come forward and speak their mind uncovers the degree of rubbish hidden under their respective carpets. In a country like Poland, it is eight years since communism collapsed, but so sensitive are Poles to their nation's history that the past continues to be a crucial dividing line. More specifically, Poles tend to differ not so much over policies but over the degree to which they supported or opposed the communist regime. Calls for "historic reconciliation" or a "historic compromise" between the two antipodes of the political spectrum, the post-communists and *Solidarity*-led organizations, have repeatedly been voiced in the run-up to the parliamentary elections in September 1997, but failed to materialize.

One legacy that all post-communist parties share is the collapse of their respective socialist regimes during 1989/90. While the nature of this implosion differed in the various countries, the challenge to confront this collapse remains the same: why did the system prove to be incapable of reforming itself without subsequently self-destructing? In other words, the *raison d'être* of post-communist parties is crucially linked to their willingness to explain the demise of a political and economic system based on the socialist ideology. This process of self-clarification includes the question how these parties are prepared to describe the political reality exercised by their predecessors. To illustrate: terms such as "Stalinist regime" or "totalitarian power" are still highly controversial classifications for members and representatives of former communist parties when having to explain the nature of government failure in Poland, Hungary or Bulgaria.

Figure 3 highlights some, but by far not all of the legacies that need, or are being addressed by post-communist parties. In saying so, it is nevertheless important to underline the fact that the arduous process of publicly debating such highly charged signposts is frequently begun involuntarily, either kick-started by parliamentary inquiries, opening of secret police files, or disillusioned former party members, who want to come to terms with their own personal involvement in past events (Ash 1997).

Table 15
Post-communist parties facing legacies of the past

PDS	Forced merger between KPD/SPD 1946 Mass uprising 17. June 1953 Berlin Wall 1961 The collapse of GDR socialism Opening of the *Stasi* files
SLD	Katyn massacre 1940 Gdansk uprising 1970 Martial law December 1981 The collapse of Polish socialism The 'Thick line' – no Lustration
MSZP	Mass uprising 1956 Execution of Imre Nagy The collapse of 'Goulash Communism'
BSP	Murder of Georgi Markov in London 1978 Bulgarization of Turkish population in 1986/87 The collapse of Zhivkov socialism

The Polish case

The legacies of the past are most explicitly addressed in two highly charged events of Polish history: (i) the Katyn forest massacre in Byelorussia in 1940, and (ii) the attempt to assess General Wojciech Jaruzelski's responsibility – let alone – guilt for the imposition of martial law on 13 December 1981. The Katyn massacre concerns Stalin's order to the NKVD to take 15.000 Polish officers from POW camps and shoot them in the aforementioned forest. Until 1990 the Soviets maintained, and Poland's Communist Party adhered to the fiction that the Nazis had committed the slaughter.

The Committee on Constitutional Responsibility of the *Sejm*, the Polish House of Representatives, probed[5] Jaruzelski in September 1992. A variety of charges were leveled against Jaruzelski, some of which had to be dropped or were supplemented in the course of the proceedings. The two most important, but equally ambiguous charges were: (i) violation of article 246 of the criminal code, i.e. abuse of power, and (ii) violation of article 123 of the criminal code, i.e. treason. As is well documented in his French memoirs[6], the general and former President of the country defended himself by arguing that martial law "saved us from national tragedy", and allowed to outmaneuver the looming Soviet intervention. The struggle over the responsibility for the imposition of martial law is a "dispute about whom to inscribe on the list of the guilty" (Rosenberg 1995, p. 239). Jaruzelski is the most prominent figure implicated in this matter. But the controversy surrounding the general ultimately extends so far to include the role of the party he once headed, the dissolved PZPR, and the post-communist SdRP.

The SLD comprises a total of 29 organizations, including the largest trade union in Poland, the OPZZ. The current leader of the SdRP is Jozef Oleksy, former Prime Minister of Poland who had to resign from that office in 1996 amidst espionage allegations for Moscow. However, when Kwasniewski was elected president of Poland, and subsequently resigned the SdRP leadership, Oleksy quickly returned to party prominence. The SLD's electoral success in 1993 has to be placed in context. Together with the PSL both parties achieved 38 percent of the vote. However, due to the specificities of the electoral law, which benefits the largest party, this share of the vote translated into a two-thirds majority of parliamentary seats. Furthermore, the then anti-Communist right as a whole, including Solidarity, won 30 percent of the vote. But no individual party crossed the five percent barrier needed to enter into parliament. In other words, the formation of an alliance strongly benefited the post-communists, while their political opponents could or would not establish a unifying umbrella in 1993.

The crucial importance of forming broad electoral alliances is illustrated by the dire effects of failing to do so. In order to prevent a repeat of the 1993 nightmare, an alliance of 36 right-of-center parties grouped around the Solidarity trade union was established for the September 1997 general election. The so-called *Solidarity Election*

Action (AWS) comprises an intriguing mix of organizations, parties and associations. These form a cocktail of political positions, which appear almost impossible to reconcile. AWS stretches from a liberal conservative wing arguing in favor of tough fiscal policies to a syndicalist wing inspired by the movement's trade union membership, in particular from the state sector. The latter endorses government support for state-owned industries and higher spending on social services. The AWS manifesto spoke of speeding up privatization and upholding "patriotic and Christian values".

The single idea that ties all groups within the alliance together is resentment of an ex-communist élite that is accused of having profited more than anyone else from Poland's post-1989 transformation. Therefore, a major element of the AWS electoral campaign consisted in calls to purge ex-communists from public life. This feature of *vendetta*-style policy-making against patronage practices of the SLD/PSL government only underlines how deep resentment continues to run in Polish politics. The AWS, which does not constitute a party, and only plans to register as such after the September 1997 general elections, is presided over by Marian Krzaklewski. Since 1991 he is the leader of the legendary trade union *Solidarnosc*, having succeeded Lech Walesa when he became President of the country. During the electoral campaign Krzaklewski repeatedly emphasized that he does not intend to become Prime Minister if AWS were to win the general elections. What should not be forgotten about Krzaklewski is the fact that as leader of *Solidarnosc* he was largely held responsible for bringing down the Suchochka reform government in 1993 when the trade union refused to support her privatization programme. Her resignation subsequently led to early general elections which the post-communists won.

The political map of Poland is unique for another reason. Until mid-1997 representatives of the SLD umbrella controlled the three core pillars of machinery of government: the presidency, parliament and the office of prime minister. This political arrangement easily created fears of a country that went from one-party rule to one-party democratic government. But this institutional specificity and the spectrum of ideological barriers existing in Polish politics since 1989/90 should not obscure the fact that a see change has taken place in terms of the generation that now forms the new post-communist élite. The President

Aleksander Kwasniewski is 42 years old. The former Prime Minister, Wlodzimierz Cimoszewicz, in office until mid-1997, is 47 years of age. Both politicians represent a new generation that has started to alter the face of Polish politics. This assessment is more convincingly argued when both representatives are compared with two neighboring politicians. Between 1990 and spring 1997 the 65-year-old Ion Iliescu was President of Romania. The former Prime Minister of Hungary, Gyula Horn, in office until July 1998, is 63 years old. Both politicians received university degrees in the Soviet Union, and held government office at a time during the seventies when Kwasniewski and Cimoszewicz chose the United States of America for study and vacation.[8]

Kwasniewski and Cimoszewicz' political roots rest in the former Communist Party Association of Polish Students. They are both known in Poland as the so-called 'boys from Ordynacka', a reference to the street in which the association had its headquarters. Even before communism's collapse in Poland the orientation of politicians like Kwasniewski reflected a mixture of pragmatism and cynicism. Kwasniewski was a junior sports minister in Poland's last communist government. Interviewed after his election as Poland's president in November 1995, he described his past career in the following words:

> From an ideological point of view, I was never a Communist. In Poland I've seen very few Communists, especially since the 1970'. I met a lot of technocrats, opportunists, reformers, liberals (Higley et al. 1996, p. 139).

In other words, such representatives did not believe anymore in communism as an ideology for government. But this state of mind of younger communist party officials does not automatically imply that they believed in its collapse either. Nevertheless, a defining element in the career of representatives such as Kwasniewski is the experience of having been thrown out of office by a combination of elections and mass protests. Hence, in order to avoid the humiliation of such an experience again, Kwasniewski and Cimoszewicz appear to have shed their Communist heritage to such an extent that their opponents are even calling them "a version of a Polish yuppie" (IHT April 8, 1996). As recently as May 1998 Cimoziewicz broke a taboo within the SLD when he argued in a newspaper article for *Gazeta Wyborcza* that the communist period between 1949 and its collapse in 1989 in Poland was characterized by "brutal and cynical exploitation of working people". The nomenclatura had to be "held responsible for leftist ideals degenerating into empty formula". Cimiziewiczc even went as far as criticizing Poland's foreign relations with the former Soviet Union, when he argued that the country's sovereignty was "succumbed under the Sowjet imperium" (Frankfurter Allgemeine Zeitung, 11.05.1998). The critical comments of a leading SLD representative, who is nevertheless *not* a member of the SdRP, are unprecedented for their clarity regarding the acknowledgement of responsibility by former communists. They may not only contribute to a necessary debate within the SLD alliance about the legacies of the past. They can equally serve as an attempt to open avenues for future collaboration between organizations grouped around *Solidarnosc/AWS* and former communists who have unequivocally broken with the past.

The Hungarian case

Gyula Horn led the *Hungarian Socialist Party* (MSZP) until September 1998. A decade earlier he was Minister of Foreign Affairs in the last communist government. Horn became known to a wider audience outside Hungary as the 'man who cut open the iron curtain'. This is a reference to his initiative to sever the barbed-wire fence at the Austrio-Hungarian border in June 1989, thus allowing less restricted travel to the West for thousands of East Germans 'vacationing' in Hungary. Horn's transition into post-1989 democratic politics was rather smooth. However, since he became Prime Minister of a coalition government with the *Free Democrats* in 1994 he has repeatedly had shed light on his personal involvement in the crushing of the 1956 uprising.

The MSZP is one of two parties competing for the legal and political succession to the former *Hungarian Communist Party* (MSZMP). The second party, virtually isolated from Hungarian political life, and not represented in any of the freely elected parliaments since 1990, is the so-called *Social Democratic Party of Hungary* (MSZDP). It was founded in January 1989. In our sample of post-communist parties, the Hungarian case is the only example where the Communist Party disintegrated, but subsequently split into two rival organizations. Since 1990 a conflict persists over who is the legal heir to the MSZMP. The durability of this controversy is explained by the implications its resolution has for the resource base of the two feuding organizations (Hankiss 1990, p. 258).

As is the case in Poland and Bulgaria (see below), the MSZP casts a wide organizational net. The trade union wing (MsZOSZ) considerably influences the party's programmatic profile and organizational resources. During the electoral campaign leading up to the second free general elections in 1994 the MSZP presented its leadership as a team of experts, with experienced professionals who knew how to run the machinery of government. This form of political positioning was a response to the first generation of dissident politicians in Hungary who were labeled as incompetent and not sufficiently prepared to carry out state administrative functions. The government of the late Joseph Antall, Prime Minister of a center-right coalition comprising the MDF, the FKgP and the KDNP between 1990 and 1994, lacked adequate middle-range professional cadres that would be capable of replacing the nomenclature milieus and running the government apparatus.

Let us further illustrate the argument. It is rather difficult to understand why Lajos Bokros, the former Finance Minister of Hungary until 1996, considers himself a socialist. His austerity package from 1994 included painful cuts in welfare provisions, hikes in higher education fees and further reductions in disposal income for large parts of the population. The programme could have been written by a Thatcherite free marketeer, but it originated from the pen of a finance minister from the MSZP, who claimed in an interview that "our task as socialists is to dismantle the state" (IHT January 6, 1996). Throughout its four-year term in office, the MSZP maintained a tight monetary policy and focused on reducing the country's external debt problem. It aggressively courted foreign direct investment with generous tax provisions. During the Horn incumbency state-owned banks were sold to foreign investors, including majority holdings.

Furthermore, the electoral manifesto of the MSZP for the 1998 general elections focused on law and order issues, sustained economic growth, and good bilateral relations with neighbouring countries, particularly Slovakia and Romania. This policy mix is seen as a major precondition for future membership of Hungary in the EU and NATO, both of which the MSZP emphatically supports. In a word, the 1998 electoral manifesto of the Hungarian socialists sought to reinforce the party's capacity to govern, while sustaining their credibility both domestically with voters and abroad with international organizations and foreign investors.

Such policy performance notwithstanding, however, the one area where the MSZP was continuously seen as being too lenient and out of touch with its constituency concerned the issue of alleged corruption and money-grabbing culture of cronyism. Ultimately, these sensitive issues, and not its policy-making record, became the defining moment in the Horn government's term in office. They further explain why the MSZP lost the general elections in Mai 1998 against the background of disillusioned voters turning their back on the socialists. In the public perception many representatives of the MSZP were seen as exempt from the austerities of the civil service. The new political class emerging around, and with the help of the MSZP leadership was regarded as hanging loose from codes and ethics, freewheeling its way through the politico-business environment. Pushing ideological imperatives of the MSZP became obsolete, taken over by a new class that found its *raison d'être* in amplifying the politics of personality and feather-bedding cronies.

The swing towards an alliance of right-of-centre parties after the May 1998 general elections was the result of the Hungarian socialists losing one third of their parliamentary seats, declining from 209 to 134 MPs. Horn's junior coalition partner, the *Alliance of Free democrats*, suffered an even worse fate. They lost two thirds of their MPs, and were reduced from a high of 70 seats in 1994 to a low of 29 representatives in 1998. The outcome of the elections thus effectively ended the era of one of the most prominent figure heads of post-communists parties in Central and Eastern Europe, G. Horn. Equally, the results confirmed a regional trend where former communists, who returned to government positions at the beginning of the nineties, have subsequently been voted *out* of office in Romania in 1996, in Bulgaria and Poland in 1997, and now in Hungary in 1998.

Turning our attention to Bulgaria, the then party leader Zhivkov initiated the brutal Bulgarization of ethnic Turks in the mid-eighties. Not only did Turkish citizens have to change their surnames into a Bulgarian version. They were equally obliged to relocate inside the country or face the alternative of forced emigration. The latter option was taken up by an estimated 60.000 Bulgarian Turks between 1985-87. The other major skeleton in the BSP's cupboard concerns the murder of the Bulgarian regime critic Georgi Markov, who was poisoned by an umbrella peak in 1978 in London. The political legacy of this crime rests uncomfortably on the shoulders of the renamed Socialist party. But to date, not even legal proceedings have been brought against any former representative of the Communist party. When the anti-communist opposition briefly governed Bulgaria in 1990/91 the state attorney's office did not dare open a legal case against Zhivkov or others in relation to the Markov murder.

When *Bulgaria's Socialist Party* (MSP) gave up the mandate to form a new government in early February 1997, the decision was seen as a significant victory against looming civil war and economic as well as financial collapse of the country. Much of the credit was attributed to two individuals: (i) the newly elected President of Bulgaria, Petar Stoyanov from the *Union of Democratic Forces* (UDF), and (ii) Mr. Nikolai Dobrev, at the time interior minister and former Socialist prime minister-designate. The former, a 44-year-old lawyer, quickly established himself as a relatively neutral figure that was clearly sympathetic to the mass protesters in the streets of Sofia calling for immediate early elections. His call for restraint in the national interest was adhered by the latter, when Mr. Dobrev defied the Marxist faction hard-liners in the BSP who wanted him to form a new Socialist party-led government at any cost. However, the prime minister-designate was aware of the danger of uncontrollable civil disorder after 30 days of mostly peaceful demonstrations, against a backdrop of hyperinflation, petrol shortages and disappearance of goods from the shops. In the end, Dobrev's agreement with President Stoyanov allowed political animosities to be channeled into more ritualized battles of an early general election campaign in Bulgaria.

The depth of polarization inside the BSP and the party's final removal from government office in April 1997 illustrated a dramatic change of events not only for Bulgarian politics, but even more so for a party who retained power directly or indirectly for six of the past eight years. The origins of the BSP's crisis lie in the failure of its successive governments to restructure a Soviet-style economy[9], which conducted 80 percent of its trade with *Comecon*, the Russian-controlled trade bloc in existence until 1989. By the same token, the political roots of the crisis rest in the incapacity of the late Andrei Lukanov (see below) to split the former communist party in 1990 shortly after the Gorbachev-style reformist pushed aside Todor Zhivkov[10], the wily communist dictator. This change from 'Zhivkov socialism' to a renamed BSP did not constitute a comprehensive U-turn in the party's ideological outlook, nor was it accompanied by a coherent restructuring of the party's apparatus, including its personnel.

In 1995 the BSP claimed to have approximately 370.000 members and over 10.000 grass-roots organizations across the country. This impressive membership base was the result of a complex web of networking between different organizations and groups forming the party architecture. Until 1997 this complexity can be untangled by highlighting two individuals who represented opposite camps of the party spectrum. Todor Lilov represented the ideological attachment to the pre-1989/90 era, while the more modern, technocratic constituency grouped around Andrei Lukanov. Together with the former *komsomol* Zhan Widenov, who subsequently became Prime Minister (see below), they formed a triumvirate at the top of the BSP.

The BSP membership and its electoral success between 1990 and 1997 were characterized by strong support from pensioners, of which over three million are registered in Bulgaria. In its electoral manifesto for the December 1994 general election the BSP emphasized a "regulated market economy" and came out in favor of "democratic socialism". Following its huge victory at the polls, the party leader, Zhan Widenov, became Prime Minister in January 1995 at the 'tender' age of 36 years. He was forced to resign from government office in December 1996. Widenov is a textbook example of post-communist élites. He ran a regional branch of the Communist youth organization during the mid-eighties. A changed party name and the attempt to alter its image transported representatives of the younger generation upward the party machinery. Widenov maneuvered his way to the party leadership with the backing not only of change-minded technocrats, but also a new class of wealthy former Communists inside the BSP. That he subsequently became Prime Minister was also the result of the instability of political coalitions in Bulgaria since 1990. In a span of five years the country had six heads of government!

When the Socialist party gained an absolute majority of the vote and seats during the December 1994 general elections, the core of its support came from four constituencies: (i) the poor(-er) classes, (ii) workers, (iii) pensioners, and (iv) the *nouveaux riches*. As is the case with other post-communist parties in Central and Eastern Europe, the view that the BSP is a party whose base rests on impoverished supporters, is a misleading interpretation. As one non-socialist MP observed in 1995:

> It's a matter of self-preservation. There are 1.000 millionaires in Bulgaria, and 5 billionaires. All of them are members of the Socialist Party, because no one else has had the access to capital, education and networks that you need to get rich here. Naturally, these people support capitalist-type policies (IHT 21.03.1995).

By keeping all factions within the renamed Socialist party, the organizational umbrella of the BSP cast a wide net. While this embrace initially proved instrumental in retaining not only political power, but simultaneously let the party appear as entrenched at the grass-roots level, the move blocked the emergence of a modern social democratic party, as happened in Hungary and Poland. With the BSP's resounding defeats - first during the presidential elections in October 1996, when its candidate, the then Cultural Minister Ivan Marazov, only polled 27.4 percent of the vote[11], and secondly at the early general elections in April 1997, when the BSP received 22.1 percent - the long-delayed reshuffling of political cards inside the party organization is now under way.

With the disintegration of the traditional Socialist electorate the Socialist party subsequently also started to fall apart. This is best illustrated by the defection of so-called "euro-leftists" and social democrats. The new grouping under the heading *'Euro Left'* was formed just before the general election in April 1997 and managed to attain 5.5 percent of the vote outright. This new party formation has manifested its willingness to become the respectable face of centre-left politics in Bulgaria by supporting various policy initiatives of the present Kostow government in parliament.

A more dramatic, and equally telling, example for the current state of the BSP is the murder of Andrei Lukanov, who was shortly prime minister in 1990. He was gunned down outside his house in Sofia in October 1996. The crime against a leading member of the party appeared to have been a contract killing in connection with disputes over corruption[12] in the BSP. Hence the biggest question mark hanging over the party apparatus during the forthcoming frustrating years of parliamentary opposition concerns how much its remaining members as well as voters are prepared to learn from a turbulent past for which they must be held politically accountable. The remaining 58 MPs of the BSP thus face a daunting, but inevitable task on the hard benches of parliamentary opposition: exercising in a convincing manner the party's capacity for internal reforms.

Questions still searching for answers

The process of remodeling is in full swing. Former communist parties' resurgence across Central and Eastern Europe has attracted the attention of those who thought that with the collapse of the regimes they once governed, the respective parties would equally face oblivion. Initially, the surprise among Western observers was considerable. How could Alexander Kwasniewski, a former communist minister, triumph in presidential elections over Lech Walesa, the historic symbol of Polish resistance against the communists? The extraordinary political comeback for a supposedly failed and buried ideology raised the fear that former communists are just 'dressed-up as sheep', gradually derailing the arduous transition process begun by those individuals, whom they once imprisoned, and who subsequently contributed to their downfall in 1989/90.

Although former communists are in power in many states across Central and Eastern Europe, their respective parties bear *more or less* resemblance to their ancestors. With the exception of Bulgaria until spring 1997, the post-communist parties under consideration in this contribution have been part of, and contributed to, democratic change. This process of establishing roots in the soil of democratic politics has advanced change within former communist parties of Hungary and Poland. In other words, the specter of post-communist parties and élites haunting Central and Eastern European transformations may make 'juicy' journalistic stereotyping, but it does not stand up to analytic scrutiny. The assumption that the collapse of communist rule involved no comprehensive turnover of élites is therefore misleading. However, there are still numerous questions searching for answers, some of which these new faces of leftist politics in Central and Eastern Europe will have to confront repeatedly.

Generalizations are a convenient means of ignoring the arduous task of sorting out the details. In countries like Poland and Hungary the old ideological labels do not apply anymore. But in others, like Serbia and Bulgaria, renamed communist parties are anything but comprehensively re-organized entities. In the latter two cases it would be fair to ask to what degree former communist parties are reincarnations of their former selves? In the case of Hungary or Poland, the applicability of old labels would only highlight their ambiguity. The MZSP calls itself "socialist" but governed in a coalition with a party comprising many former dissidents, the *Alliance of Free Democrats* until June 1998. The coalition's austerity policies have been subject to rigorous criticism domestically, but the measures proposed could also have come from the hands of Margaret Thatcher.

Sometimes comparisons with the 'odd man out' can underline the essence of an argument. Post-communist parties have a common ancestry in the communist parties, which ruled the former Soviet Empire. But do they share anything else, and are they still of one family with the parties that continue to hold power in China, North Korea, Vietnam or Cuba? In the case of Poland and Hungary, the post-communists' return to power has not derailed economic reform nor stopped the process of privatization. However, some of the emphasis, sequencing and procedures have changed, such as the introduction or extension of voucher privatization. But on the whole the SLD in Poland and the MZSP in Hungary have maintained the commitment to bring their respective economies in line with a view to joining the European Union. This achievement is reflected in the countries' credit risk ratings improving since 1994.[13] The SLD, once the champion of capitalism's losers in Poland, announced itself during the 1997 campaign for the general elections as the party of winners. Its slogan was "Good Today – Better Tomorrow".[14]

However, at the micro-economic level the assessments are not as positive. Ex-communist parties in government have repeatedly been accused to confound public and private interests, for muddling up favoritism with competition, thus re-enforcing a system of cosy patronage in sectors such as banking, telecommunications and commercial trade. Furthermore, post-communist parties will have to illustrate their adherence to the rules of the democratic game when it comes to handing over governmental power as a result of losing general elections. In the case of the Bulgarian BSP this credibility test took some time. While it accepted the outcome at the ballot box, the BSP needed convincing to agree to early elections in 1997, which the party's leadership knew they would lose. By contrast, the Polish case illustrates that during the 1997 general election campaign nobody assumed that the SLD would not voluntarily hand back power in case it were to lose the elections. The same holds for the Hungarian MZSP, which lost the general election in 1998. This assessment serves to draw attention to the following argument: eight years after their predecessors' demise most post-communist parties not only take part in the democratic process, but essentially adhere to its parameters.

This view leads to the question if there is a danger of *recommunization* of these parties? The short answer is a clear no. Leninist ideology and organizing principles are not only scrapped from the parties' platforms, but equally rejected in their essence. In particular the Polish and Hungarian examples illustrate the transformation from a party of apparatchiks into one of career-minded technocrats. By the same token, post-communist parties have observed the institutional architecture of democratic politics. Moreover, they have used this architecture to their advantage when mobilizing grass-roots support, organizing electoral campaigns and initializing activities in the machinery of government and/or parliament. Even in the case of Bulgaria the BSP leadership has no appetite for a return to Zhivkov's brand of socialism. During their time in office until 1997 many top-level representatives of the BSP have economically benefited from democratization and marketization à la Widenov, Lukanov etc. Their successful transformation from nomenclature milieus into capitalists has paid dividends under the umbrella of democratic politics. A further indicator that recommunization is not on the cards concerns the support which post-communist parties proclaim in favor of joining the EU, and in most cases also entering NATO. The leaderships of the SdRP in Poland and the MZSP in Hungary emphatically embrace both goals. Only the BSP clearly rejects a possible membership bid for NATO, but is more open to EU integration.

Finally, a word of caution is appropriate. One should not fall prone to getting overly excited about post-communist parties. In particular the political debate in Germany in the run-up to the general elections in September 1998 sometimes gives the impression as if the PDS is the most important issue in current German politics. It is not at all. Post-communist parties are neither the torchbearers of social democracy in Central and Eastern Europe, nor do they represent gloom and doom scenarios for the region's further development. Post-communist parties have been voted into office. But as the examples of Bulgaria and Poland illustrate in 1997 as well as the recent case of Hungary, the electorate has equally voted them out of office.

This turn of events tells us as much about the parties' electoral appeal as it highlights the existence of substantial electoral volatility. Voters in Central and Eastern European countries ruthlessly punish those parties in government who fail to deliver on their economic and social promises, lack a coherent reform concept, and appear to be more concerned with enriching themselves then serving the citizens. The events in Bulgaria at the beginning of 1997 are a telling reminder of such means of democratic punishment. To further prove the point, consider the following: In Hungary all three general elections held since the start of the transformation process in 1989/90 have produced a change of government at the hands of voters' authority. This form of exercising sovereignty at the ballot box signifies that stable, long-term party preferences cannot be taken for granted by those holding elected office in Central and Eastern Europe, no matter what political affiliation they represent. While the profile of political parties is maturing and parliaments in Poland, Hungary, the Czech Republic and Bulgaria are increasingly characterized by a narrowing of the number of parties represented therein, the pendulum swings from one side to the other are still eye-catching. Such an observation underlines nothing less then a process of consolidation of the democratic polity. The turbulent environment in which this takes place will persist for some time, but normality is gaining currency, and the clock cannot be turned back.

Notes

1   Since 1995 the Polish SdRP has an observatory status in the *Socialist International.*

2   Apart from the SdRP, the PSL is the second reconditioned communist-era party in Poland. The party chairman, Waldemar Pawlak, was Prime Minister in 1992. Its attempt to shed the communist stigma as a former bloc party affiliated to the PZPR is a controversial undertaking. In the government coalition with the SLD, the party positioned itself as a Christian-social organization with predominant support in the rural areas of Poland. This endeavor has nevertheless not prevented the PSL from being labeled a "water melon", i.e. green on the outside, but red inside.

3   This line of argument links with Wiesenthal's (1996) so-called *'Transformation durch Vereinigung'* which he applies to the overall transformation process of East Germany.

4   The leader of the Russian Communist Party, Gennady Zyuganov, urged the army in 1992 to fight "the destructive might of rootless democracy". When the party was outlawed in 1992, Zyuganov helped set up a so-called "National Salvation Front". In 1993 the CPRF was legalized. Apart from their fervent nationalism, this Salvation Front was united by its hostility to the dismantling of the former Soviet Union. Zyuganov is a clear cut example of the new communist bigwigs who are typically officials which held modest posts in the central apparatus or in regional committees of the old Soviet party. A revealing, but equally worrying characteristic of Zyuganov is his unconcealed admiration for Stalin and his contempt for Gorbatshev.

5   In 1993 Jaruzelski faced another parliamentary investigation into his role of the shooting of Gdansk protesters during the 1970 riots.

6   His memoirs were published in France in 1992. See Jaruzelski (1992).

7   Transforming the AWS alliance into a party under the proposed name *Social Movement AWS* will be a testing experience. The process implies that the different organizations currently comprising the electoral alliance will have to renounce their independent existence and come under the organizational umbrella of formal party structures. The broader issue this challenge addresses concerns the question if it is at present possible in Poland to unite liberal, conservative and national-catholic groups as well as the Solidarity trade union into one comprehensive Christian-democratic party organization. It remains to be seen if the post-Solidarnosc camp can achieve such a merger. The example its protagonists encouragingly point to is the German CDU, which successfully united diverse right-of centre branches into one common party tree after 1945.

8   Kwasniewski studied economics and earned money as an unregistered worker in Sweden to pay for a trip to America for the bicentennial celebrations in 1976. Cimoszewicz is a law graduate from Warsaw University and won a Fulbright scholarship to Columbia University in the early eighties. It is a telling reminder of his experiences overseas that Cimoszewicz, on his return from the United States, retreated to the family pig farm in eastern Poland for four years. He turned it into a model operation – of the capitalist kind. He maintains that he was "tremendously" successful financially.

9   A typical example is the Soviet-era Kremikovtsi steel plant north of Sofia, which employs over 16,000 workers and is a chronically loss-making company. Until mid-1997 each BSP led- or influenced government continued to bail out such loss-making enterprises.

10   Zhivkov was the longest ruling head of state and Communist party leader in the former Warsaw pact. Gorbatshev once termed him the "Chinese emperor of Bulgaria". In September 1992 he received a seven-year prison sentence from the Supreme Court because of self-enrichment. He served part of the sentence in domestic

confinement until the same court acquitted him after the post-communists again took office in 1995.

11 These results reflected the first round of presidential elections. Since neither candidate gained an absolute majority, the two front-runners, P. Stoyanov and I. Marazov, faced a deciding round of voting one week later, which the former comfortably won with a 60 percent share of the vote. The stinging defeat for Bulgaria's former communists was a vote of no confidence in the then governing BSP. The Socialist party lost votes to protest candidates, including George Ganchev of the *Bulgarian Business Bloc*, who polled 22.8 percent in the first round. In total the BSP is said to have lost one million of its voters, many of who did not vote at all. The first warning signs of eroding electoral support for the governing socialists came when the BSP lost close to 700.000 votes during the local government elections in the fall of 1995.

12 Lukanov was a member of the Communist party since 1965. He was deputy Prime Minister under the former party leader T. Zhivkov. After the removal of Zhivkov, in which Lukanov is said to have had a major hand, he became Prime Minister in February 1990, and was confirmed in this position at the first free elections in June of the same year. He was forced to resign in November 1990. The precise nature of the corruption claim is not yet known. Some observers have spoken of foreign-exchange dealings with which parts of the BSP were associated. While he did not hold political office again, Lukanov became managing director of the Russian-Bulgarian energy company *Topenergy*, which earned him the term "red millionaire" inside the Socialist party.

13 The European credit rating agency *IBCA* awarded Poland a so-called BBB long-term sovereign rating in March 1997. At the height of the general election campaign the US rating agency *Moody's Investors Service* issued a report in which it argued that an election victory by AWS could lead to unfavorable economic policy changes. Hence, a continuation of the existing SLD/PSL coalition was the implicit position of *Moody's*. This public endorsement of post-communist parties through an international credit rating agency became a heated bone of contention in an otherwise modest election campaign.

14 The metaphorical meaning of this slogan is reproduced by the telling transformation of the old Communist Party headquarters into the financial banking center of Warsaw, including the vibrant stock exchange.

References

Ash, T. G. (1997), *The File. A Personal History*, Harper Collins: London.

Bastian, J. (1995), 'The *Enfant Terrible* of German Politics: The PDS Between GDR Nostalgia and Democratic Socialism', *German Politics*, Vol. 4, No. 2, pp. 95-110.

FAZ = Frankfurter Allgemeine Zeitung, June 17, 1997, '*PDS würdigt den Aufstand vom 17. Juni*'.

----, March 17th, 1998, '*Spenden, die nach Gelatine riechen*'.

----, May 11th 1998, '*Cimiszewicz kritisiert linke Parteien*'.

Gillespie, R., Waller, M. and Lopez Nieto, L. (1995/eds.), *Factional Politics and Democratization*, Frank Cass: London.

Hankiss, E. (1990), *East European Alternatives*, Clarendon Press: Oxford.

Higley, J., Kullberg, J. and Pakulski, J. (1996), 'The Persistence of Postcommunist Elites', *Journal of Democracy*, Vol. 7, No. 2, pp. 135-147.

IHT = International Herald Tribune, March 21, 1995, '*In Sofia, Can Youth Succeed Where Experience Failed?*'

----, January 6, 1996, '*Communism's Resurgence: Separating Hype From Reality*'.

----, April 8, 1996, '*Boys From Ordynacka Are Turning to the West*'.

Jaruzelski, W. (1992), *Les Chaines et le Refuge: Memoires*, Editions Jean-Claude Lattes: Paris.

Kowalczuk, I.-S. (1996), ''Faschistischer Putsch' – 'Konterrevolution' – 'Arbeitererhebung': Der 17. Juni 1953 im Urteil von SED und PDS', in Eckert, R. and Faulenbach, B. (eds.), *Halbherziger Revisionismus: Zum postkommunistischen Geschichtsbild*, Olzog: Landsberg am Lech, pp. 69-82.

Meuschel, S. (1992), *Legitimation und Parteiherrschaft in der DDR*, Edition Suhrkamp: Frankfurt a.M.

Rosenberg, T. (1995), *The Haunted Land. Facing Europe's Ghosts After Communism*, Random House: New York.

Segert, D. and Machos, C. (1995), *Parteien in Osteuropa. Kontexte und Akteure*, Westdeutscher Verlag: Opladen.

Waller, M., Coppieters, B. and Deschouwer, K. (1994/eds.), *Social Democracy in a Post-Communist Europe*, Frank Cass: Ilford, Essex.

Wiesenthal, H. (1996/ed.), *Einheit als Privileg. Vergleichende Perspektiven auf die Transformation Ostdeutschlands*, Campus Verlag: Frankfurt a.M.

Zubek, V. (1995), 'The Phoenix Out of the Ashes: The Rise to Power of Poland's Post-Communist SdRP', *Communist and Post-Communist Studies*, Vol. 28, No. 3, pp. 275-306.